A CALL TO ACTION

INSPIRE

/in´spī(ə)r/

TO FILL (SOMEONE) WITH THE URGE
OR ABILITY TO DO OR FEEL SOMETHING.

GAIL E. DUDLEY

Dedication

I DEDICATE THIS BOOK to the viewers and listeners of *News in Motion*.

To my dearest friends—you know who you are—and to my parents and siblings who understand my passion for civic engagement and advocacy, thank you for cheering me on.

I am forever grateful to my wonderful husband, Kevin, and my adult children, Alexander and Dominiq. Thank you for unwaveringly supporting my work.

—Gail

Table of Contents

Foreword

IMAGINE A WORLD WHERE kindness and determination pave the way for change. That's the world Gail Dudley invites us into with her inspiring book, *INSPIRE: A Call to Action.*

I first met Gail in 2015 at a campaign-training workshop at the John Glenn School of Public Affairs at The Ohio State University. Despite our different political stripes, there was a spark of shared hope—a belief that ordinary people could make a real difference.

During the years, I saw politics becoming more about tearing down than building up. So I started focusing on what truly matters: trust, transparency, and building relationships.

Gail's book echoes my belief that civic engagement isn't just about fixing potholes. It's about giving the voiceless a platform, about building bridges across divides, and about sparking the power of hope within ourselves and our communities.

Gail's story is a reminder that we all have the power to make a difference. So grab your courage, open your heart, and step into the world of bold moves and boundless possibilities. This book is your guide!

—Nancy Bocskor

* * *

Passionate about redefining political leadership, Nancy Bocskor has empowered generations of public servants. Having led fundraising efforts for members of Congress and trained candidates across the country, she now inspires individuals to unlock the power of personal relationships and forge new paths to public service.

Bocskor brings her expertise to the classroom as an adjunct professor at The George Washington University's Graduate School of Political Management, guiding students through the intricacies of "Fundraising & Budgeting." Her groundbreaking book, *Go Fish: How to Catch (and Keep) Contributors*, offers practical wisdom for building lasting donor relationships.

Introduction

DO YOU YEARN FOR daily inspiration that can uplift your spirit while keeping you informed about important issues?

Welcome to the world of *INSPIRE: A Call to Action*, a unique blend of daily inspiration with headline news and civic engagement. Created from the inspirational messages shared on *News in Motion with Gail*, this book is your daily dose of empowerment.

As the world becomes increasingly focused on negativity in news and politics, this devotional offers a refreshing perspective. Each day, you can turn to a new page, read a short inspirational message, take notes, and shift your mindset towards a positive and empowering perspective. Once you have reached Devotion 150, begin again.

Some days you'll find that a single word can significantly improve your outlook. You even have space to jot down your thoughts and the date in response to each devotional. It's your personal space for reflection, strategizing, and recording how you plan to participate in civic engagement or which cause you will contribute to, be it through monetary donations or volunteer hours. This section can help you track your journey toward finding inspiration while making bold moves.

At the core of *INSPIRE: A Call to Action* is the belief that daily inspiration can motivate individuals to recognize their potential and encourage them to pursue their dreams. In these pages you'll discover a renewed sense of purpose, empowerment, and a call to action that can help you transform your life.

More than just a collection of inspiring messages, this book seeks to drive you toward active participation in your community and beyond, inspiring you to take an engaged role in shaping society. By absorbing these daily messages, you'll gain the strength to approach each day with hope and determination.

As you read, you will find that some devotions in this book may be similar to others. I did so intentionally. Just keep reading one or two a day. Sometimes we have to be repetitive to drive a point home. Agreed?

The goal of this book is to transform you into a well-informed, engaged, and active citizen in your daily life, particularly in civic engagement. We hope it will inspire you to go beyond merely consuming news and encourage you to be an active participant in creating positive change.

News in Motion, the grassroots media platform that inspired this book, strives to stimulate civic engagement. It delivers headline news, promotes voter education, and encourages participation in the electoral process. Its uplifting messages aim to motivate and empower, inspiring you to take meaningful actions in your community.

PEOPLE. PRAYER. POLITICS. PROSE.

As I persist at the crossroads of humanity, faith, and governance, I'm continually reminded that I'm not in control; it is God who reigns supreme. He has called me to this moment, to serve people through various means, whether it be through my writings, social media posts, emails, videos, or intimate one-on-one conversations. God has granted me the privilege to approach Him in spirit and truth, interceding on behalf of fellow warriors, raising their prayer requests, and worshiping His name with reverence. The Lord allows me to engage in humble petitions, urging Him to heed our supplications.

In this space, God has permitted me to delve into research and explore the complex political environment. For many years I have carried a deep desire to educate voters and inspire unregistered individuals to exercise their right and duty to engage in local and national politics. The reality is that everything holds a political dimension, as we perpetually navigate and manage power and resources. Both the Old and New Testaments in Scripture provide room for God's people to partake in issues concerning the common good, community welfare, and justice for all. Take a look at Micah 6:8 which calls us to, "to be fair, just, merciful, and to walk humbly with your God" (TLB).

I cannot escape the conviction that God has given me the grace and authority to be a voice amid the disparities I encounter as a politically moderate Christian Black woman. What inequities do you confront? Take a moment today for introspection and share your reflections with someone you regularly connect with. Don't be afraid to have the conversation.

Tensions are on the rise. Partisan politics are driving deeper divisions, with those on the right vehemently opposing those on the left, and vice versa. In the midst of this, the center ground is becoming a breeding ground for more unhealthy and damaging rhetoric. The never-ending stream of negative discourse is pushing ordinary people to shout at and over each other, often resorting to unhelpful soundbites. Racial tensions have escalated to levels not seen since the unrest of the 1960s. People are taking to the streets to mobilize and protest; however, there are others who oppose these movements with harmful intentions by fabricating incidents and using law enforcement to enforce their biases.

Don't let the naysayers distract you. They are stationed to discourage us. It's time to be the modern-day Harriet Tubman and execute a strategic plan of action, regardless of those who may oppose us. Reflect on James Weldon Johnson's composition, "Lift Every Voice and Sing." As you ponder the song, let's elevate our voices and forge ahead, drawing inspiration from the certainty that bold actions pave the way to triumph. May we persist in our march, confident in the victory that accompanies our daring moves.

Individuals who may have once been fearful or silently observant are now finding their voices and taking a stand. In this ever-changing landscape, one must exercise divine wisdom and devote themselves to prayer to hear the voice of God. God is speaking. The question is, "How will we respond?" I believe that Jesus applauds us for raising our voices and taking a stand.

I confess, I am weary. I'm utterly exhausted. But I cannot halt my forward momentum. "I look up to the mountains; does my strength come from mountains? No, my strength comes from God, the Maker of heaven, earth, and mountains" (Psalm 121:1-2, MSG). While we're in the struggle, we must tap into God's power and wisdom and practice self-care. Recognize when to step back and recharge. Someone else will step in and continue the forward movement. Remember, we're in this together.

A Note from the Author

EVERY BOOK RELEASE CARRIES a moment of uncertainty. Unexpected circumstances led to significant delays for this book, postponing its release by over a year. The fear of the unknown nearly prevented it from reaching your hands. Nevertheless, I chose to confront my fear and embrace my calling, and through my journey, I aim to inspire you to do the same.

Second Timothy 1:7 reminds us that we possess a spirit of power, love, and a sound mind. Fear may accompany our calling, but it doesn't define it. As the host of *News in Motion* (www.GailDudley.com), I encounter this fear daily, but I persist because I understand that this is my calling.

This book doesn't promise to eliminate fear but rather to encourage you to move forward with courage despite it. I hope this book awakens something within you and propels you beyond the status quo, even if you have to do it while experiencing fear.

Maintain your focus on your assignment, ignoring any naysayers who may challenge you. Remember that obedience to God and His instructions is of utmost importance.

Come alongside me within the pages of this devotional to explore the transformative potential of making courageous strides, whether you're an entrepreneur, business owner, advocate, philanthropist, organization founder, community organizer, corporate executive, politician, teacher, the everyday citizen, minister, or quite simply, any individual within this world.

Are you ready? Let's find inspiration and make some bold moves.

PART 1

Devotions

DEVOTION 1

Embracing Boldness

DON'T JUST SIT THERE, embrace boldness.

In life, we often find ourselves at crossroads, facing decisions that require courage and determination. It is during these moments that making bold moves becomes essential. However, the path of boldness is not always easy. It demands stepping out of our comfort zones, overcoming fear, and relying on God's guidance.

> "Be strong and courageous. Do not be afraid or terrified because of them, for the LORD your God goes with you; he will never leave you nor forsake you" (Deuteronomy 31:6).

God calls us to live with boldness and courage. He reassures us that He is always with us, guiding and supporting us through every step of our journey. When we trust in God's presence, we can step out in faith and make bold moves. Take a moment to reflect on the times when fear held you back from making a bold move. How might your perspective change if you fully embrace God's promise to be with you?

Let's take a look at Esther, a young Jewish woman chosen to be the queen. When her people faced annihilation, Mordecai, her cousin, urged her to approach the king and intercede on their behalf. This required boldness and courage, as anyone who approached the king without being summoned risked their life. Yet Esther chose to make a bold move. She fasted, prayed, and entered the king's presence, risking everything. Through her boldness, God used Esther to save her people from destruction.

Bold moves often come with risks, challenges, and uncertainties. However, when we align our hearts with God's truth and seek His guidance, we can find the strength to overcome our fears. Making bold moves requires trusting that God is in control and that He will equip us for the battle and the journey. Remember, God does not call us to live in fear but to embrace boldness. What bold move is God calling you to make?

Dear heavenly Father, thank You for being our ever-present guide and source of strength. Help us to overcome our fears and step out in faith when making bold moves. Grant us wisdom, discernment, and courage to follow Your will, knowing that You are with us every step of the way. May our lives be a testament to Your faithfulness. In Jesus' name. Amen.

Be Inspired: Make Bold Moves

_____

_____

_____

_____

_____

_____

_____

_____

_____

_____

_____

_____

_____

_____

_____

_____

_____

_____

_____

_____

_____

_____

_____

_____

_____

DEVOTION 2

Write the Vision

WHAT'S YOUR VISION FOR making bold moves in your life? Do you have a dream you've longed to pursue but are uncertain about where to begin? The Bible instructs us to "write the vision and make it plain." As an example, I'd like to share my own journey in the hope that it will inspire you to start crafting your own vision.

Over the past couple of years, I've grappled with aligning all the different callings God has placed on my heart for this season of my life. It seemed challenging to connect media, news, civic engagement, advocacy, publishing, and consulting, and even writing all of this down felt overwhelming.

You might wonder if I'm scattered in various directions. But it's God who has gifted me with these abilities. Just as there are different seasons in life, there are times when we can use various gifts. So after spending time in prayer, I took pen to paper and began to write my vision. I immersed myself in what God was revealing, and through this exercise, I hope you will find clarity for your own journey as well.

1. Find a quiet and comfortable place where you can focus without distractions.
2. Take a few deep breaths to center yourself and quiet your mind.
3. Pray and ask God for guidance, wisdom, and clarity as you seek to discover your vision.

4. Take out a pen and paper or open a document on your computer.
5. Write down the question: "What is the vision that God has for my life?"
6. Reflect on this question and allow your thoughts to flow freely. Write down any words, phrases, or sentences that come to mind.
7. Don't worry about structure or editing at this point. Simply let your thoughts and inspirations flow onto the page.
8. If you feel distracted or influenced by negative thoughts, take a moment to pray for God's silence and ask for His voice to be the only one you hear.
9. After you have written down your initial thoughts, take a moment to thank God for His guidance and for speaking to your heart.
10. Keep your vision private for now. Set it aside and take time to reflect and pray further before sharing it with others.

Remember, this process may take time, and it's important to be patient and open to God's leading. Trust that He will reveal His vision for your life in His perfect timing.

"Write down the revelation and make it plain on tablets so that a herald may run with it. For the revelation awaits an appointed time; it speaks of the end and will not prove false. Though it linger, wait for it; it will certainly come and will not delay" (Habakkuk 2:2-3).

Be Inspired: Make Bold Moves

_____
_____
_____
_____
_____
_____
_____
_____
_____
_____
_____
_____
_____
_____
_____
_____
_____
_____
_____
_____
_____
_____
_____
_____
_____
_____

DEVOTION 3

What's Your Strategy?

"Once when they had finished eating and drinking in
Shiloh, Hannah stood up" (1 Samuel 1:9).

IN THE STORY, CHAPTER 1, verse 3 states, "year after year."
Elkanah loved Hannah, but despite this, she felt frustrated
and hurt due to her rival provoking her. One day after a meal,
Hannah stood up with a strategy in mind.

It's important to focus on building a strategy for what
you desire, rather than dwelling on what you lack. Start by
asking yourself questions about your purpose, mission, and
vision, and what you need to achieve your goals. Consider
areas where you can grow and your available resources, as well
as the people in your circle of influence and who you'll invite
to the table. Pray about the timing of when to share your
strategy with others.

Developing a strategy to stay inspired and make bold
moves is indeed crucial for achieving our goals and fulfilling
our purpose. Here's a suggested framework to help you build
your strategy:

1. **Define Your Purpose, Mission, and Vision.** Take
   time to reflect on your purpose in life, your mission,
   and the vision you have for your future. Ask yourself
   meaningful questions, such as:

- What is my ultimate purpose in life?
- What mission am I called to fulfill?
- What is the vision I have for my life and the impact I want to make?

Write down your responses and craft a clear and concise statement for each of these areas.

2. **Identify Goals and Needed Resources.** Identify the specific goals you want to achieve that align with your purpose, mission, and vision. Determine what you currently have and what you need to acquire or develop.

3. **Cultivate Growth and Leverage Resources.** Reflect on areas where you can grow and develop to enhance your ability to make bold moves. This may involve acquiring new skills, seeking mentorship, pursuing educational opportunities, or expanding your network. Surround yourself with individuals who believe in your vision and challenge you to push beyond your limits.

4. **Overcome Opposition and Stay Focused.** Just as Hannah faced opposition from Eli, it's important to anticipate that there may be challenges and people who may try to discourage or deter you from your path. Stay true to your passion and purpose, remembering that God's calling on your life is greater than any opposition you may face. Seek strength and wisdom from Christ.

5. **Pray for Discernment and Timing.** Invite God into your strategy-building process. Pray for discernment and guidance, seeking His wisdom in every step.

Remember, building a strategy takes time and requires flexibility. Remain open to adjustments and redirection along the way as God leads you on your journey. Stay inspired, keep your focus on what you desire, and trust that with God's guidance, you can make bold moves and accomplish great things.

Hannah's journey to taking a stand took years, and when she did, she faced opposition from Eli the priest, who mistook her for being drunk. In your own strategy, there may be people who try to deter you, but it's important to stay true to your passion and purpose. Have faith in God's promises and be bold enough to set your strategy in motion.

Be Inspired: Make Bold Moves

_____

_____

_____

_____

_____

_____

_____

_____

_____

_____

_____

_____

_____

_____

_____

_____

_____

_____

_____

_____

_____

_____

_____

_____

_____

_____

_____

DEVOTION 4

Prosper. Hope. Future. Plan.

AS BELIEVERS, WE CAN trust that God has great plans for each one of us. His plans are rooted in His perfect wisdom, unconditional love, and desire for our ultimate well-being. When we face uncertainty or difficulties, it can be challenging not to question these plans. However, embracing trust and focusing on the potential benefits that God's plans may bring can provide us with hope and assurance.

When we think about the words "prosper," "hope," and "future" in the context of God's plans, we are reminded of the abundant blessings and promises that He has in store for us.

God desires for us to prosper, not only in material wealth but also in every aspect of our lives. His definition of prosperity goes beyond financial gain. It encompasses spiritual growth, emotional well-being, healthy relationships, wisdom, and fulfilling our purpose in Him. As we align ourselves with God's plans, He will provide for our needs and bless us abundantly, according to His perfect wisdom.

"Beloved, I pray that all may go well with you and that you may be in good health, as it goes well with your soul" (3 John 1:2, ESV).

God's plans infuse our lives with hope. Even in the midst of challenges and uncertainties, we can hold onto the hope that comes from knowing God is in control. His plans are filled with promises of redemption, restoration, and eternal life. As we place our trust in Him, He renews our hope, enabling us to persevere and find strength in Him.

"For I know the plans I have for you, declares the LORD, plans for welfare and not for evil, to give you a future and a hope" (Jeremiah 29:11, ESV).

In God's plans, our future is secure. He has a purpose and a calling for each one of us. As we surrender our lives to Him and seek His guidance, He unfolds His plans for our future step-by-step. However, we must be patient and wait on God's directions. Our future is not determined by chance or circumstance but by the loving design of our heavenly Father. He holds our future in His hands and promises to guide us every step of the way.

"And we know that for those who love God all things work together for good, for those who are called according to his purpose" (Romans 8:28, ESV).

That's the key. It is knowing, "All things work together for good." As we embrace God's plans, let us remember that they are founded on His love, wisdom, and perfect timing. We can trust that His plans will bring about the fulfillment of His promises as we align our hearts with His will. May the words "prosper," "hope," and "future" serve as a reminder of the incredible blessings that await us in God's plans for our lives.

Each season has opportunities of prosperity, hope, and future planning. We have a responsibility to seek God, trust the process, and lean in with our whole hearts. Our hope comes from knowing that God has individual plans for each of us and is working on our behalf to propel us towards our appointed future.

Even if we don't fully understand God's plans for us at this moment, we can trust that He is guiding us towards our future. It is important to recognize even the small plans that are revealed to us, and to take steps to trust in God's unfolding plan for our lives.

Be Inspired: Make Bold Moves

DEVOTION 5

Do Not Be Anxious

THE BIBLE ENCOURAGES US not to be anxious. In Philippians 4:6-7, it says:

> "Do not be anxious about anything, but in everything by prayer and supplication with thanksgiving let your requests be made known to God. And the peace of God, which surpasses all understanding, will guard your hearts and your minds in Christ Jesus" (ESV).

In the ongoing political climate of challenges and uncertainties, it's easy to succumb to anxiety. However, the Bible reminds us not to be anxious but to turn to prayer and thanksgiving. In Philippians 4:6-7, we find a profound message of hope and comfort.

God invites us to bring all our worries, concerns, and requests to Him in prayer. He doesn't want us to carry the heavy burden of anxiety on our own. Actually, anxiety has no place in our lives. God calls gives us, power, love, and a sound mind as we read in 2 Timothy 1:7.

Release the fear and anxiety and pray. Pray knowing that God is with you. Period. When you pray, couple it with a spirit of thanksgiving. Even in difficult times, there are things to be grateful for. When we express gratitude to God, it shifts our perspective. It reminds us of His faithfulness in the past and strengthens our trust in His provision for the future.

Instead of allowing anxiety to overwhelm us, we can trust in God's plans and promises. He is in control of all things, working for our good, even when we can't see it. By surrendering our worries to Him, we make room for His peace to guard our hearts and minds.

Today, if you face any challenges and uncertainties of life, remember Philippians 4:6-7. Turn to God in prayer, with a heart full of thanksgiving, and experience the peace that only He can provide. Cast your anxieties upon Him, for He cares for you. Trust in His faithfulness, and let His peace guard your heart and mind, no matter what circumstances you may encounter.

May I pray for you? If so..

Lord, we invite You into this space. May we encounter Your grace, mercy, and love all the days of our life. Jehovah Jireh, You are indeed our provider. Shower down upon us Your favor today and always. Equip us to stand strong and to cast all of our burdens upon You. May we acknowledge who we are and embrace Your love. In Jesus' name. Amen.

Be Inspired: Make Bold Moves

DEVOTION 6

Yes, I Can

LOOK IN THE MIRROR and declare, "Yes! I can!"

"I can do all this through him who gives me strength" (Philippians 4:13).

Sometimes we may feel like we don't have the energy to get through the day. During these moments, we can turn to Jesus and draw strength from Him to keep going. Although it may be tough and draining, it's important to remember that we can do anything through Christ who strengthens us.

Let's consider food insecurity. At this writing, food insecurity, according to the USDA, is the lack of consistent access to sufficient food for a household's active and healthy living. This can be a temporary or prolonged state, serving as a measure of those unable to afford food. Over 34 million people in the United States, including 9 million children, experience food insecurity.[1]

I firmly believe that many children who experience difficulties in the classroom may be doing so because of hunger. Hunger can undoubtedly impact a child's ability to comprehend and learn effectively. However, some want to place an

---

[1] *Feeding America*, "Hunger in America," https://www.feedingamerica.org/hunger-in-america/food-insecurity.

unfair label upon children, when it could be as simple as ensuring they have a healthy diet on a regular basis.

Understanding this, it's crucial for us to pause and reflect and allow the Holy Spirit to prompt us to ask ourselves, "What role can I play in identifying those who are hungry within my community so that I can contribute to providing food for those facing anxiety due to food shortages, allowing them to experience peace?"

It is within our power to cultivate a mindset of trust, faith, and surrender to God, which can help alleviate anxiety and bring about a sense of peace. Rely on God's strength. Be patient with yourself and give yourself grace. Trust that as you intentionally choose to embrace the words, "I can do all this through Him who gives me strength," your weakness will shrink and God will help you experience His peace and provide the strength you need to navigate any challenges you may face.

Let's declare and decree today: "With God's strength, I can face and conquer anything that comes my way, including helping those who may face food insecurity."

Be Inspired: Make Bold Moves

DEVOTION 7

Rejoice

"Rejoice in the Lord always. I will say it again: Rejoice! Let your gentleness be evident to all. The Lord is near. Do not be anxious about anything, but in every situation, by prayer and petition, with thanksgiving, present your requests to God. And the peace of God, which transcends all understanding, will guard your hearts and your minds in Christ Jesus. Finally, brothers and sisters, whatever is true, whatever is noble, whatever is right, whatever is pure, whatever is lovely, whatever is admirable—if anything is excellent or praiseworthy— think about such things. Whatever you have learned or received or heard from me, or seen in me—put it into practice. And the God of peace will be with you" (Philippians 4:4-9).

CONSIDER THE WORD, "REJOICE." Sit with it for a moment. Now visualize a life filled with joy, free of anxiety, and filled with gratitude. Imagine having peace of mind and heart by focusing on what is true, right, pure, lovely, admirable, excellent, and praiseworthy. Consider starting your day by practicing what you have learned from reading the Bible. Embrace the peace of God and live life with delight.

How would embracing joy and the peace of God even in the midst of challenges and world situations change your life?

Take inspiration from this message today and rejoice in the goodness of life. For fun, use #Rejoice on all your social media platforms and spread the joy. Let's go!

Be Inspired: Make Bold Moves

DEVOTION 8

Finding Healing for Our Communities

IN REFLECTING ON THE narrative of the woman with the issue of bleeding, a powerful lesson emerges. She had suffered for twelve long years, seeking healing from countless sources, but it was only when she reached out to touch the hem of Jesus' garment that her affliction was finally resolved.

There are many among us who are broken, carrying the weight of their pain. If you find yourself in this situation, I want to speak directly to you. While you may not be able to physically touch the hem of His garment, remember that you can reach out to Him in your heart. Jesus is here, right beside you, and He's always within your reach. Let's pause for a moment and invite Jesus in. Let's extend an invitation to God right now. As a matter of fact, make it a standing invitation. Lord, we invite You...

In our communities, just like the woman's affliction, there are issues that seem to cause continuous suffering and pain. Instead of merely attempting to halt the bleeding, it's essential to seek solutions that address the underlying challenges. This calls for resilience, determination, and a commitment to finding healing for our wounded communities. While the bleeding may persist, we can work together to address the root causes of pain and suffering.

In times of trial, remember that Jesus is always with us. Just as the woman found healing through her persistent faith and determination, we too can find solutions and relief for our communities. Trust in His presence and never lose hope, for His grace is sufficient to guide us through even the most challenging times.

Be Inspired: Make Bold Moves

_____

_____

_____

_____

_____

_____

_____

_____

_____

_____

_____

_____

_____

_____

_____

_____

_____

_____

_____

_____

_____

_____

_____

_____

_____

_____

_____

_____

DEVOTION 9

Play the Music

WITHOUT FAIL, THERE'S A melody that can stir my spirit, swiftly altering the atmosphere around me. It has the power to elevate my already joyful mood or gently guide me out of a somber state when I'm feeling down. These moments bring back memories of my mother humming hymns while she worked in the kitchen when I was a little girl. It was her way of dealing with whatever weighed on her heart. She'd start with a soft hum, gradually adding lyrics.

Sometimes it was the soothing "What a Friend We Have in Jesus," and at other times, it could be the soul-stirring "Oh, the Blood of Jesus." She'd even transition to "Great Is Thy Faithfulness" or a heartfelt gospel song that poured out from the depths of her soul. Raised in the church, I find myself humming and then singing hymns now that I am an adult when I'm doing everyday tasks, like washing the dishes.

Playing music has a remarkable ability to shift the atmosphere and uplift our spirits. When we engage in music, whether by playing an instrument or listening to our favorite songs, it has the power to shift the atmosphere by moving us to a different emotional and mental state. The melodies, rhythms, and harmonies can evoke deep emotions, bringing comfort, joy, or even release.

Music has a unique way of touching our souls, connecting us to the depths of our being. It can encourage and inspire us, offering a respite from the challenges of life and infusing us with renewed energy and motivation. Whether we play music ourselves or simply allow it to permeate our surroundings, it can create an atmosphere that fosters positivity, creativity, and a sense of peace. So let the power of music surround you, embrace its melodies, and let it guide you to a place of encouragement and inspiration.

The next time you need to lift your spirit or shift the atmosphere, try singing a hymn such as "O the Blood of Jesus." It's a powerful song that gives strength in your weakest moment. When you sing, you'll find your mood automatically improves, and the problems that once consumed you will fade away.

Take this as today's inspirational message—no matter what's going on in your life, singing a song can help. Create a playlist for moments you need uplifting.

Be Inspired: Make Bold Moves

DEVOTION 10

Be Strong and Courageous

DEUTERONOMY 31:6 SAYS, "BE strong and courageous. Do not be afraid or terrified because of them, for the LORD your God goes with you; He will never leave you nor forsake you."

Being strong and courageous in difficult situations requires a mindset of resilience and determination. It involves facing challenges head-on, even when fear and uncertainty try to hold us back. To be brave, we must first acknowledge our fears and insecurities, understanding that bravery is not the absence of fear but the willingness to move forward despite it.

Cultivating inner strength involves trusting in God's promises and relying on His guidance. It means embracing discomfort and stepping outside of our comfort zones, knowing that growth and transformation often occur in those spaces. Surrounding ourselves with a support system of loved ones who uplift and encourage us can provide the strength we need.

Prayer, self-reflection, and seeking wisdom from others can also help us find the courage to face difficult situations. Ultimately, being strong and courageous is a daily choice—a decision to believe in our own capabilities and to trust in God's faithfulness as we navigate life's challenges with bravery and grace.

How will you be brave today?

Be Inspired: Make Bold Moves

DEVOTION 11

Walk in Freedom

"It is for freedom that Christ has set us free. Stand firm, then, and do not let yourselves be burdened again by a yoke of slavery" (Galatians 5:1).

YOU HAVE THE FREEDOM to live your life unburdened by the opinions and expectations of others. In order to truly experience freedom, it is vital to practice forgiveness and release the weight of life. Recognize and embrace the power of God and the power God gives you, refusing to allow anyone or anything to enslave you in toxic situations.

Protect yourself by letting go of feelings of guilt or shame and embracing a life of freedom. It is important to remember that true liberation is found in Christ, who offers us His unconditional love and redemption. Through His grace, we can experience complete freedom, unshackled by past mistakes and empowered to live boldly and authentically.

Be Inspired: Make Bold Moves

DEVOTION 12

Firm and Secure

"We have this hope as an anchor for the soul, firm and secure" (Hebrews 6:19).

BEING HOPEFUL, FIRM, AND secure in our everyday lives is essential for navigating the ups and downs of life with confidence and peace.

Hope allows us to see beyond our current circumstances and believe in a brighter future. It fuels our dreams and fuels our resilience, reminding us that there is always a reason to keep going.

Firmness enables us to stand strong in our values and convictions, even when faced with opposition or challenges. It gives us the courage to stay true to ourselves and our beliefs, unwavering in the face of adversity.

Security comes from knowing that we are deeply loved and cared for by God. It is rooted in our faith and trust in His unwavering presence and faithfulness.

With hope, firmness, and security, we can embrace each day with a sense of purpose, confident that we are not alone, and that we have the strength to overcome obstacles. By nurturing these qualities in our lives, we can cultivate a deep sense of peace, joy, and contentment, allowing us to thrive in every season.

Be Inspired: Make Bold Moves

DEVOTION 13

Hold onto Your Power

STOP GIVING YOUR POWER away.

Stop giving your power away.

Stop giving your power away.

I want to encourage you to hold onto your power and not give it away to others. Your power lies within you, waiting to be acknowledged and unleashed. Embrace your unique strengths, talents, and abilities, and recognize the incredible potential that resides within you. Trust in your own judgment and discernment. Believe in your worth and the validity of your voice. Remember that you have the right to set boundaries and prioritize your well-being.

Don't allow others to diminish your power or influence your decisions. Instead, cultivate a deep sense of self-belief and confidence, knowing that you have the strength to navigate life's challenges and create the future you desire. You possess the power to shape your own destiny and live a life that aligns with your values and aspirations. Embrace your power, hold it close, and let it guide you to a place of empowerment and fulfillment.

You have the power to reclaim whatever you may have previously given to someone else who has spoken contrary to what God has told you to do. It is common for us to feel deflated or defeated when others tell us we are incapable of pursuing what God has already called us to. However, it's time to put an end to allowing such influences to occupy space in our lives.

When we surrender our power, we align ourselves with others instead of aligning with God. Let us make the decision to reverse that pattern and cease giving away our power. Take a moment to reflect on your journey thus far and ask yourself, "Whom have I given my power to, and what steps can I take to reclaim it?" By taking ownership of your power once again, you can confidently pursue the path God has laid before you.

I love what one of our viewers on *News in Motion* shared on his Facebook post. He said that we need to hit the delete button for people who have been speaking negatively. Identify those toxic relationships that you may have and find a loving way to get out. You don't have to stay somewhere you don't want to stay; however, we have been conditioned to think that we just must go with it. No, you don't have to go with it. Raise your voice and have a say to the life you are living. Let's hit the delete button.

Be Inspired: Make Bold Moves

_____
_____
_____
_____
_____
_____
_____
_____
_____
_____
_____
_____
_____
_____
_____
_____
_____
_____
_____
_____
_____
_____
_____
_____

DEVOTION 14

What Do You Want Me to Do for You?

GOD, WE WANT THE right to vote regardless of skin color, socioeconomic status, disability, worldviews, educational level, or gender. This is what we ask for all of us.

I think about the story of Bartimaeus in Mark 10:46-52. In the midst of a bustling crowd, Bartimaeus, a man who had never seen the world around him, stood waiting. His physical blindness didn't obscure the vision he held within his soul—a vision of an encounter with Jesus, the beacon of hope and healing. Bartimaeus didn't merely vocalize his desire; he fervently pleaded for clarity and light in his darkness. He cried out loudly, undeterred by the potential judgments of others.

In response to his heartfelt plea, Jesus, ever perceptive, posed a simple yet profound question: "What do you want Me to do for you?" This moment underscores the importance of being specific in our prayers. Bartimaeus's example encourages us to express our needs, desires, and hopes with clarity and boldness. Thus, as we navigate our own journeys, we must emulate Bartimaeus's persistence and unwavering faith, not hesitating to share with God what we want Him to do for us.

This practice of bold and specific prayer aligns our hearts with His divine plan and timing, allowing us to trust in His ability to answer according to His wisdom, which often surpasses our understanding. Like Bartimaeus, let us cry out to God, undeterred and specific in our petitions, knowing that He listens and responds according to what is best for us.

Here's my cry, and I refuse to allow anyone to silence me. Maybe it is yours as well. God, we, the people, all people, want the right to vote. Period.

42

Be Inspired: Make Bold Moves

_____

_____

_____

_____

_____

_____

_____

_____

_____

_____

_____

_____

_____

_____

_____

_____

_____

_____

_____

_____

_____

_____

_____

_____

_____

_____

_____

DEVOTION 15

Enjoy

TODAY IS ALL ABOUT having some fun.

Having fun regardless of what is happening in the world around us is a testament to the power of joy and resilience. It means embracing a mindset of positivity, seeking moments of laughter, and finding delight in the simple pleasures of life. It is an intentional choice to not let external circumstances dictate our internal state.

Having fun amidst challenging times is not about ignoring or trivializing the struggles; rather, it is a conscious decision to nurture our well-being and find moments of respite. It is a reminder that even in the midst of chaos, there is still beauty, laughter, and enjoyment to be found.

Having fun allows us to tap into our creativity, connect with others, and find a sense of freedom. It brings a renewed energy, lightness of heart, and a fresh perspective. Let us embrace the power of having fun, allowing it to be a source of strength, refreshment, and a reminder that joy can coexist with the world's challenges.

Personally, I find immense joy in my life. I have no reservations about expressing my laughter, whether I'm in a library, coffee shop, or amidst shopping. I smile with my entire face. I laugh with my full body. Embracing self-love to a great extent, I make it a point to find humor in any situation, as it lifts me out of any feelings of misery

If you were to ask those who truly know me, they would affirm that laughter is an integral part of who I am. It doesn't matter what is happening around me; I am unafraid to burst into laughter, even within the confines of a church. I am not afraid to be silly and have fun.

I encourage you to inject some fun into your day. I assure you, it has the power to transform any situation. Simply let go, have fun, and let laughter be your companion today.

Politics, worldviews, the everyday shenanigans will be there for you tomorrow.

Be Inspired: Make Bold Moves

DEVOTION 16

Be a Blessing

"Bless those who persecute you; bless and do not curse"
(Romans 12:14).

BLESSING OTHERS AND REFRAINING from cursing them is a
profound way to cultivate a spirit of love, compassion, and
unity. When we choose to bless others, we extend kindness, encouragement, and support, uplifting their spirits and
contributing to their well-being. It involves speaking words of
affirmation, offering acts of service, and genuinely caring for
their needs. By doing so, we foster an environment of positivity and nurture meaningful connections.

On the contrary, cursing others with harsh words or ill
intentions only perpetuates negativity, division, and harm.
When we choose to bless instead of curse, we reflect the heart
of God, who calls us to love our neighbors as ourselves. Let
us strive to be intentional in our words and actions, spreading
blessings and fostering a culture of grace, understanding, and
unity in our interactions with others.

Take a moment to join me on a journey and contemplate the idea of extending blessings to those on the opposite
side of the political spectrum or who may have a different
worldview. I genuinely believe that embracing this kind of
profound transformation is essential to foster unity and create
an atmosphere where we can welcome others to help reshape
our current political landscape.

Be Inspired: Make Bold Moves

DEVOTION 17

Give

THE CONCEPT OF GIVING is woven deeply into the tapestry of our faith. In Luke 6:38, we're presented with an essential truth: "Give, and it shall be given unto you; good measure, pressed down, and shaken together, and running over" (KJV).

This verse carries a profound message about the reciprocity of giving. It reminds us that when we open our hearts and hands to give generously, we not only share our blessings with others but also position ourselves to receive in abundance. The act of giving isn't solely about tangible gifts or financial contributions; it encompasses the kindness, love, and compassion we extend to those around us.

The principle of giving is a reflection of God's abundant grace and His divine economy. He encourages us to be open-handed and openhearted, assuring us that when we give freely, without hesitation or reservation, we create space for blessings to flow back into our lives. It's not a transaction in which we give to receive; rather, it's a testament to the overflowing abundance of God's love and provision.

Just as a farmer sows seeds with the expectation of a bountiful harvest, our acts of giving are akin to planting seeds of goodwill, hope, and positivity in the lives of others. And just like those seeds grow and yield a rich harvest, our giving, be it time, resources, or support, has a ripple effect that multiplies and returns to us in ways we may not even anticipate.

This principle of giving is not limited to material possessions; it extends to giving our time, our talents, and our love.

When we live with open hearts, giving freely, we find ourselves in harmony with God's intention for our lives. Our faith isn't just about receiving; it's about recognizing our capacity to give.

As we journey through life, let's remember the beautiful promise in Luke 6:38. Give generously, without hesitation, and without the expectation of return. In this act of selflessness, we align ourselves with God's abundant grace and open the door to His blessings, which are poured out in good measure, pressed down, shaken together, and running over. Give, and in doing so, receive the abundant love and grace of our heavenly Father, for it is in giving that we truly reflect His heart.

GIVE

Be Inspired: Make Bold Moves

DEVOTION 18

In But Not Of

"If the world hates you, keep in mind that it hated me first. If you belonged to the world, it would love you as its own. As it is, you do not belong to the world, but I have chosen you out of the world. That is why the world hates you. Remember what I told you: 'A servant is not greater than his master.' If they persecuted me, they will persecute you also. If they obeyed my teaching, they will obey yours also" (John 15:18-20).

WHILE IT'S EASY TO get caught up in the chaos of the political landscape, always keep in mind that as individuals, we may reside in this world, but our values and principles should set us apart. Approach every situation with unwavering confidence, guided by your higher beliefs and convictions.

Yes, we might live in this world, but as believers, our hearts dance to a different beat. We're like cosmic adventurers, striding through the mundane with a touch of divine flair. We navigate earthly landscapes, yet our spirits soar beyond the limitations of this realm. We wear the cloak of earthly existence, but our souls radiate with a heavenly glow. We embrace laughter, joy, and the simple pleasures of life, knowing that they are glimpses of the abundant life that awaits us.

We bring a splash of vibrant colors to the grayscale of routine, injecting wonder, love, and compassion into every encounter. We dance to the rhythm of grace, spreading a contagious sparkle wherever we go. So let's live fully, embracing the adventure of being in the world but not of this world, painting the canvas of existence with a palette of divine joy.

I am one who believes that God couldn't care less about our politics. Yes, I say all the time, the Bible is political, but God cares more about your heart and loving your neighbor than about what side of the aisle you are on. Right?

Be Inspired: Make Bold Moves

DEVOTION 19

Call to Action: Community

BEING IN COMMUNITY IS a call to action, an invitation to stand alongside those who have been marginalized and silenced. It requires us to listen with empathy, to open our hearts to their stories and experiences. It means challenging the systems and structures that perpetuate inequality and advocating for justice. In community with the oppressed, we acknowledge our shared humanity and the intrinsic worth of every individual. We offer a safe space where voices can be heard, wounds can be healed, and strength can be found.

It is a commitment to use our privilege, resources, and influence to uplift and empower those who have been pushed to the margins. Together, we forge a bond of solidarity, weaving a tapestry of compassion, love, and resilience. In being community with the oppressed, we not only bring hope and healing, but we also become transformed ourselves, enriched by the diversity and wisdom that emerges from our collective journey.

Be Inspired: Make Bold Moves

_____
_____
_____
_____
_____
_____
_____
_____
_____
_____
_____
_____
_____
_____
_____
_____
_____
_____
_____
_____
_____
_____
_____
_____
_____
_____

DEVOTION 20

As Long As I Have Breath

"Because he inclined his ear to me, therefore, I will call on him as long as I live" (Psalm 116:2, ESV).

AS LONG AS YOU have breath, live with purpose and intention, following the instructions of God. Each breath is a reminder of the precious gift of life and the opportunities it presents. Promise to use your breath to speak words of kindness, encouragement, and love. Use it to stand up for justice, to advocate for the marginalized, and to be a voice for the voiceless. Be intentional and use your breath to create, to inspire, and to bring joy to others.

Tell yourself, that as long as you have breath, you will strive to make a positive impact on the world around you, leaving a legacy of compassion, integrity, and grace. Agree to cherish every breath as a chance to grow, to learn, and to deepen your connection with others and with God.

With each inhale and exhale, be reminded of the incredible power within you to make a difference, to spread light in the midst of darkness, and to leave a lasting imprint on the hearts and lives of those you encounter. As long as you have breath, be committed to living a life that matters, embracing the fullness of each moment and savoring the beauty and possibilities that life offers.

As long as you have breath, use your voice to advocate for others. Let your words stand for something meaningful, and start by exercising your right to vote. If you're not yet a registered voter, you can register at www.vote.us.

Be Inspired: Make Bold Moves

DEVOTION 21

Don't Quit

THE INSPIRATIONAL MESSAGE TODAY is simple yet powerful: don't quit. Keep doing what you love, even if no one is watching. Do it for yourself, for your own uplifting and fulfillment. Pursue your passions and purpose with excitement and dedication. Let your heart sing with joy as you engage in what gives you life. Don't quit, even when you long for an audience or validation.

Remember that God has ordered your steps, and you are walking in alignment with His calling for you. Whether you have a large audience or just an audience of one, give your best and persevere. Start with small beginnings and trust that your efforts will bear fruit. Don't give up, no matter the circumstances or the size of the audience. Keep pursuing your dreams, enjoying the journey, and making an impact. Remember, the true reward comes from staying true to yourself and following God's leading.

Be Inspired: Make Bold Moves

DEVOTION 22

Be Anchored

IN TIMES LIKE THESE, it is crucial to be anchored. The hymn "Anchored" has resonated within me, reminding me of the need for a Savior and an anchor. We must be very sure of Who holds our hand and Who holds tomorrow. It is essential to be certain of the steps we take, the words we speak, and the convictions within our hearts.

Personally, I strive to be certain of my relationship with the Savior. Whether I'm in prayer, walking the neighborhood, or engaging with the news, I want to be deeply sure that I am hearing God clearly and discerning what to share and how to share it. I seek balance, fairness, and a strong sense of assurance.

When discussing the challenging realities of the world, such as the impact of the coronavirus back in 2020, I want to convey a message that instills hope and empowers individuals to take charge of their health. I want to be sure that when I offer assistance to others, they trust in my sincerity and reliability.

Similarly, as we distribute food to those in need, I want to be absolutely certain that it reaches those who require nourishment, not being allocated for operational costs. When it's time to speak up, I want to be so sure that my words align with the truth of God's message.

In times like these, we undoubtedly need a Savior, and we need to be resolutely anchored in our faith. Let us be very sure, unwavering in our trust, and grounded in the hope that our actions and words reflect His love and grace.

What about you? Are you ready to be anchored?

Be Inspired: Make Bold Moves

_____

_____

_____

_____

_____

_____

_____

_____

_____

_____

_____

_____

_____

_____

_____

_____

_____

_____

_____

_____

_____

_____

_____

_____

_____

_____

_____

_____

_____

_____

DEVOTION 23

Seek Forgiveness and Release the Person

SEEKING FORGIVENESS AND EXTENDING forgiveness are transformative acts of grace and healing. When we recognize our own faults, mistakes, and the ways we may have hurt others, we must have the humility to seek forgiveness. It requires acknowledging our wrongs, taking responsibility, and genuinely repenting. By doing so, we open the door to restoration and reconciliation.

Similarly, extending forgiveness to others is a powerful act of love and compassion. It involves letting go of resentment, releasing the burden of holding grudges, and choosing to forgive, even when it's difficult. Forgiveness doesn't mean condoning or forgetting the hurt caused, but it allows us to break free from the chains of bitterness and find freedom.

Both seeking forgiveness and forgiving others are transformative acts that promote healing, restore relationships, and pave the way for personal growth and reconciliation. Let us embrace the power of forgiveness, both in seeking and extending it, as we strive for reconciliation and foster a culture of grace, love, and understanding.

Presidential elections can be emotionally charged, often leading to actions and words that divide us. Despite our differences, let's actively seek common ground to bridge those divides. It's essential to both offer and be receptive to forgiveness. The elections of 2016 and 2020 have left a lasting impact, causing rifts even within families, where some remain estranged. Is it not time to move beyond those elections, extend forgiveness, and release the hold they have on us? Although it may have been a challenging journey, now is the moment to place our trust in God and focus on what lies ahead. Do you agree?

Be Inspired: Make Bold Moves

_____

_____

_____

_____

_____

_____

_____

_____

_____

_____

_____

_____

_____

_____

_____

_____

_____

_____

_____

_____

_____

_____

_____

_____

_____

_____

_____

_____

_____

DEVOTION 24

I Will Live

"I will not die but live, and will proclaim what the LORD has done. The LORD has chastened me severely, but he has not given me over to death" (Psalm 118:17-18).

BELOVED, YOU WILL LIVE, with an unwavering purpose that beats within your heart. Despite the challenges, setbacks, and moments of doubt, you carry within you a resilience and strength that will guide you through the darkest of nights. Life's journey may be filled with unexpected twists and turns, but you possess an innate ability to adapt, learn, and grow.

Embrace each new day with hope, for it holds endless possibilities and opportunities for you to thrive. Your dreams, aspirations, and passions are not in vain. They are the driving force behind your existence, propelling you forward to create a life that is meaningful and fulfilling.

Remember, you have within you the power to overcome, to rise above any obstacles that come your way. So believe in yourself, embrace the challenges, and cherish the moments of joy. Embrace the truth that you will live a life that is uniquely yours, leaving a positive impact on the world around you. Live fully, love deeply, and seize each precious moment with unwavering determination. You will live, and your life will be a testament to your strength, resilience, and the limitless possibilities that lie before you.

Be Inspired: Make Bold Moves

DEVOTION 25

Good Trouble

"Peace I leave with you; my peace I give to you. Not as the world gives do I give to you. Let not your hearts be troubled, neither let them be afraid" (John 14:27, ESV).

JOHN LEWIS WAS A visionary and courageous leader who dedicated his life to the pursuit of justice and equality. He believed in the power of "good trouble"—the notion that standing up against injustice and inequality requires bold action and a willingness to disrupt the status quo.

Throughout his life, Mr. Lewis fearlessly marched, protested, and spoke out against racial discrimination, voting rights violations, and social injustices. He faced numerous arrests, physical attacks, and setbacks, yet he never wavered in his commitment to creating a better world. His unwavering belief in nonviolent resistance and his resolute determination to make a difference inspired generations to rise up and fight for what is right.

Mr. Lewis taught us that change is possible when we are willing to get into "good trouble," to challenge unjust systems, and to advocate for the marginalized and oppressed. His legacy lives on as a beacon of hope, urging us to never shy away from speaking truth to power and to always strive for a more just and inclusive society.

Let us continue to honor his memory by carrying on the spirit of "good trouble" in our own lives, pursuing justice with unwavering resolve and making a lasting impact on the world around us.

What good trouble are you stirring up?

Be Inspired: Make Bold Moves

_____

_____

_____

_____

_____

_____

_____

_____

_____

_____

_____

_____

_____

_____

_____

_____

_____

_____

_____

_____

_____

_____

_____

_____

_____

_____

_____

DEVOTION 26

A Woman's Right to Fight: Exercise Hope and Vote Your Voice

BORN IN THE POST-CIVIL War South in 1915, Inez Peek Pryor was a fierce, proud, Black woman who believed in participating in her civic duties, empowering the women around her to do the same by standing strong on the principles, morals, and values that shaped their lives. Inez never worked a day in her life except to serve as a poll worker during the elections. Clad in a string of pearls, a pillbox hat, a skirt that hit her knees with heels to match, a stylish cardigan, and flawless makeup with her red lipstick poppin', she would carry her ever-present pocketbook and walk boldly to the polling location determined to take her place and serve.

Inez Peek Pryor was also my grandmother. Her legacy instilled in me the very same fire that drove her to the polls, the same fire to equip others to use their voice, to vote with pride and conviction. Her grace and confidence (and red lipstick) remain etched in my memory even now as I fight for the very same rights.

Just four years after the birth of my grandmother, Congress passed the Nineteenth Amendment on June 4, 1919, granting women the right to vote. On November 2, 1920, more than 8 million women throughout the United States voted in elections for the first time. However, the Nineteenth Amendment did not include Black women, who were effectively banned from voting until forty-five years later with the passage of the Voting Rights Act of 1965.

Knowing this, I am perplexed at the number of eligible women in 2022 who have chosen not to register to vote or cast a ballot if registered. The US Census Bureau reports that only 68.2% females 18 years and older are registered voters, and of that, only 63.0% voted in 2020.

And it won't necessarily get easier. Between January 1 and December 7, 2021, at least 19 states passed 34 laws restricting access to voting. More than 440 bills with provisions that restrict voting access have been introduced in 49 states in the 2021 legislative sessions.

Haven't we as women been silenced long enough? Aren't we tired of fighting to be heard? Raise your voice (and your vote) for those who are disabled, elderly, and the marginalized. Cast your ballot for our children, to end poverty, for accessible healthcare, affordable housing, unjust evictions, student loan debt forgiveness, living wages, voting rights, to end child hunger, and reduce food insecurity. Just a few things for starters.

Tap into the power and strength of the women before us from 1920 and 1965 and even now, who marched, protested, and exercised their right. Even in the face of grave danger, women like Inez Pryor never stopped believing they would get the chance to vote.

Ready to register? Visit:

www.USA.gov
www.Vote.org
www.Vote.gov
www.rockthevote.org
www.whenweallvote.org
www.iwillvote.com

Once you are registered, consider becoming a poll worker to help keep all polling locations open, even in the marginalized areas. Visit www.eac.gov.

Every voice matters. Every vote makes a difference.[2]

---

[2] Article originally placed in *Hope for Women Magazine*, February 15, 2022, https://www.hopeforwomenmag.com/hope-for-women-magazine/2022/2/2/a-womans-right-to-fight-exercise-hope-and-vote-your-voice.

Be Inspired: Make Bold Moves

DEVOTION 27

Encourage

"Therefore encourage one another and build one another up, just as you are doing" (1 Thessalonians 5:11, ESV).

DON'T FORGET TO BUILD up yourself while you are building others.

As you devote yourself to building up others, it is crucial not to forget the importance of building yourself as well. Just as you pour into the lives of those around you, remember to nourish your own soul, spirit, and well-being. Take time to invest in self-care, self-reflection, and personal growth. Build yourself up by cultivating a positive mindset, embracing your strengths, and addressing areas that require improvement.

Engage in activities that bring you joy, inspire creativity, and foster a sense of fulfillment. Nurture your physical, emotional, and spiritual health through exercise, rest, and spiritual practices. By prioritizing your own growth and well-being, you will be better equipped to support and uplift others.

Remember, building yourself is not selfish; it is an essential part of becoming a more whole and impactful individual. So as you continue to build up those around you, make sure to build yourself up as well, ensuring that you are nourished, empowered, and ready to make a positive difference in the lives of others.

Be Inspired: Make Bold Moves

_____

_____

_____

_____

_____

DEVOTION 28

Just Because

THE INSPIRATIONAL MESSAGE TODAY is rooted in the powerful words of Luke 5:5: "But because you say so, I will let down the nets." In this passage, Simon Peter demonstrates obedience and trust in Jesus' words, despite his own doubts and weariness.

Similarly, we are called to step out in faith and follow the guidance of God, even when circumstances seem challenging or discouraging. It's time for us to rally together, signaling for others to come and join us in our mission. Each one of us has unique skills and talents to contribute to this collective effort.

As a community, we possess a wealth of knowledge and expertise that can be utilized to make a positive impact. Let us tap into the potential within the community and offer our support, whether through curriculum development, proposal writing, legislative advocacy, or simply offering prayers and encouragement to families in need.

We must not give up or throw in the towel. Though we may feel tired, we are still equipped with the energy and purpose to continue this important work. We have a responsibility to be the light in this dark world, showing love, compassion, and hope to those around us. With God leading the way, we can press forward, knowing that our efforts are making a difference in the lives of others.

Let us remember: because He says so, we have work to do. Together, let us be the beacons of light, bringing healing, transformation, and love to those in need.

Be Inspired: Make Bold Moves

_____
_____
_____
_____
_____
_____
_____
_____
_____
_____
_____
_____
_____
_____
_____
_____
_____
_____
_____
_____
_____
_____
_____
_____

DEVOTION 29

Get Unstuck

DREAMS AND VISIONS ARE the sparks that ignite our entrepreneurial spirit and creative souls. They carry us beyond the
confines of mundane routines and propel us towards a life
filled with purpose and passion.

From a young age, I observed my dad and grandpa
absorbing their work ethic and entrepreneurial drive. Their
painting and washing walls ventures ignited a spark within
me, and even as a little girl, I eagerly approached clients for
payment with the invoice in hand. The traditional desk job
held no allure for me. Despite my efforts to find fulfillment
in that setting, I felt myself losing sight of who I truly was.
Deep down, I knew that I was meant to be an entrepreneur, a
visionary, and a creative force.

To break free from feeling stuck, it is crucial to identify and
embrace our strengths and weaknesses. By understanding our
unique abilities, we can leverage our strengths and seek support
or development in areas where we may be less proficient. This
self-awareness empowers us to navigate our entrepreneurial
journey with confidence, harnessing our creative prowess and
visionary mindset to pursue our dreams. Let us boldly embrace
our true selves, unlock our potential, and embark on a path
that aligns with our passions, talents, and aspirations.

Be Inspired: Make Bold Moves

DEVOTION 30

Celebrate Your Accomplishments

TAKE A MOMENT TO celebrate your accomplishments, both big and small. In a world that often emphasizes the pursuit of goals and the next challenge, it's important to pause and acknowledge how far you've come. Celebrating your accomplishments allows you to recognize your hard work, dedication, and personal growth. Whether you've achieved a major milestone or made progress towards a long-term goal, it's a reason to celebrate.

Take what I call a "life look" and reflect on the challenges you've overcome, the skills you've developed, and the positive impact you've made. Celebrating your accomplishments not only boosts your confidence and motivation but also provides an opportunity to express gratitude for the support and opportunities that have contributed to your success.

So raise your mimosa glass and toast to your accomplishments, treat yourself, or simply take a moment to bask in the joy of your achievements. You deserve to celebrate and savor the fruits of your labor.

Advocates, please take some time to step back from your work. When you're ready, return to the movement and continue moving forward.

Be Inspired: Make Bold Moves

DEVOTION 31

The Shift

PREPARE TO SHIFT. THERE is a shifting happening, and we must be ready to adapt and embrace it. It's natural to find comfort in our familiar routines and hold onto what we have, but God is calling us to release certain things and prepare for change.

The time for shifting is upon us. I believe God is looking upon His faithful servants, commending them with a well done, and signaling that a shift is coming. While I cannot provide a specific date or time, I am certain that change is on the horizon. Many of us have weathered the challenges of the pandemic, inflation, keeping our heads held high, and maintaining an "I can do" attitude. We know that Jesus reigns, and God is saying, "I am about to shift you."

Let us not resist this shift. Embrace it wholeheartedly, for if we resist, we may be delayed rather than denied. As we move forward, God may ask us to slightly adjust our course, urging us to turn just a little to the left while continuing to forge ahead. It is in that direction that He will open doors, providing us with opportunities that will cease the oppression we may have experienced. Furthermore, our famine is coming to an end. God assures us that our season of lack and scarcity is over.

As we shift, we should recognize that God trusts us. He sees our faithfulness and knows that we will steward the abundance He bestows upon us well. This shifting will bring about an overflowing abundance of wisdom, knowledge, health, and yes, even wealth. However, wealth should not be limited to financial riches alone. There is something greater at play here.

Seek God for yourself, inquire about the shift, and discover the ways to navigate this outpouring of blessings. Now is the time to live into this abundance, to lean into it, and to fully enjoy it. But let us not be greedy. We are called to share this abundance with others, to extend a helping hand and uplift those around us.

Do not resist the shift. Embrace it, for it is incredibly good. It is a manifestation from heaven that will rain down upon us, bringing forth a joy that is indescribable. The famine is over, and now we can live in the fullness of God's promises. Thank You, God. Let us step into this new season with gratitude and a willingness to share the blessings we receive.

Be Inspired: Make Bold Moves

DEVOTION 32

Faith and the System

RECEIVE THIS MESSAGE CENTERED on the profound concept of faith.

Faith, as described in the Bible, is the substance of things hoped for and the evidence of things not seen. In these trying times, it's imperative to cling to our faith and live by it, instead of relying solely on what our eyes can perceive. Let me share a story that exemplifies the incredible power of faith.

I'm about to make a statement that may make you tremble, whether you agree or not. As I write this, my parents are both in their late 80s. My mother is considered homebound and unable to move about. In light of all we've been through, I, like many others, have exclaimed, "Healthcare is the biggest scam in America." There, I've said it. We've contributed to a system for fifty, sixty, or even more years, only to discover that we still can't access the necessary help when needed.

If you own your home, good luck receiving medical assistance, especially if you're on Medicare. You can either deplete your savings, pay your bills out of pocket, or risk being discharged from a nursing facility. I've personally gone through this with my parents. We've had to challenge rulings, file appeals, and, in most cases, come out unsuccessful.

The decisions made by the people sitting in their offices, be it in a building or their homes, are based on the wording used in these appeals. They seem to overlook the fact that patients may be unable to climb stairs, or that they live alone or with someone who is facing similar challenges. What's going on?

Yet, I still had faith.

I began my research. I came across the following, doing what I could to be an advocate and assist my parents.

For an elderly person to be eligible for nursing home care, assisted living, adult foster care, or in-home care from Medicaid, they must have limited income and assets. To prevent candidates from simply giving away their money or resources to qualify for Medicaid, the federal government implemented the "look-back period". This is a set period of time prior to the individual's application during which the Medicaid administering agency reviews all the financial transactions that the senior has made. If a transaction is found to be in violation of the look-back period's rules, the applicant will be assessed a penalty. Penalties come in the form of a period of time that the applicant is made ineligible for Medicaid. This means they will not be able to receive care services paid for by Medicaid for a certain number of months or, sometimes, even years.

A Medicaid applicant is penalized if assets (money, homes, cars, artwork, etc.) were gifted, transferred, or sold for less than the fair market value. Even payments to a caregiver can be found in violation of the look-back period if done informally, meaning no written agreement has been made. Please note, asset transfers by the applicant's spouse can also affect the applicant and can result in a Medicaid penalty period for the applicant. The reason for this penalty period is that these assets could have been used to help cover the cost of long-term care, had they not been gifted or transferred.

In 49 of the 50 states, the length of the look-back period is 5 years (60 months). As of 2020, the one exception to this rule is California, which has a 2.5 year (30 month) look-back period. The look-back period begins the date that one applies for Medicaid. For instance, if an elderly individual completes an application for Medicaid on July 15, 2018, the look-back period begins on that date and goes back 5 years to July 15, 2013 (or in California, back to Jan. 15, 2015).[3]

Make this make sense.

Okay, Medicare must be better, right? Wrong!

As the author of this book, I know this firsthand the moment the system stops paying for my loved one's care. It was as though they said, "It's time for you to go. Either pay privately or leave." Harsh, isn't it? It is.

We often rely on the social workers and insurance personnel at these facilities. They inform us of what's about to happen, and depending on our knowledge or lack thereof, we comply. We notify our support network for pickup, even though we might find ourselves back in the same place within hours, weeks, or a few short months. So why release the individual in the first place? Doesn't it cost more?

The key is to ask questions. Every family member must have an advocate or two or three, all speaking the same language in the same voice. In fact, one voice, one advocate, is best, especially when dealing with the process.

---

[3] Expert Reviewed By: Joshua Iversen, President, Syzygy Financial LLC, "Medicaid's Look-Back Period Explained: Exceptions & Penalties," Paying for Senior Care, last modified October 30, 2023, https://www.payingforseniorcare.com/medicaid/look-back-period.

Did you know you can appeal a decision? I didn't until I started asking questions. Allow me to digress with a backstory for a moment.

My incredible mom was in the hospital at the age of 86 and was transferred after several days to a rehabilitation facility. A month earlier, she was admitted to the hospital and then transferred to a rehabilitation facility. Yes, it's a cycle.

The second time around, my sibling and I wondered, *Why release her just to end up in the same place again?* I took action, it might have been failed action, but it was action nonetheless.

After speaking with the social worker at the facility, I was more confused than helped. I thought to myself, *Isn't the social worker the patient's advocate?* I guess not always. I informed the social worker that I would make my way up to the facility to discuss a plan of action. I grabbed my iPad, a notebook, and a folder after speaking with an attorney who shared valuable wisdom. Together, we prepared a statement to have signed by a notary who met me at the facility.

The statement read, "I, [my mom's name], grant my daughter, Gail Dudley, permission to access all my records, including but not limited to notes from physical therapy sessions, case worker and social worker discussions, notes from doctors and nurses visits, and any other communications, including electronic versions. I authorize you to grant Gail Dudley the authority to access and review all records between [the facility], government officials (including communications with Medicaid and/or Medicare) regarding my health, to Gail Dudley."

Signed. Dated. Notarized.

Bookmark this page in the book, as you may need it some day.

This is where I learned how one can appeal a decision. If you get turned down, no problem; there is a second-level appeal as well.

So I went to work on behalf of my parents and my siblings, drafting the second-level appeal after my parents were denied the first appeal.

Words matter. Language matters.

Let's start with these simple but powerful words.

"[Name] does not have a safe discharge plan." Believe it or not, those words can change the narrative quickly.

Don't stop there. While those words can slow the process in your favor, learn what else to say and what not to say.

In speaking with an advocate, they informed me that custodial care is rarely approved. Whereas one may think to appeal based on home modifications, the lack of 24/7 care, bedroom setup, and other emotional and general needs to keep someone alive and cared for, stop. Believe it or not, these things are not considered important. Here's where you have to focus. I received the following advice from someone who cares.

These revisions make the text more readable and clear, maintaining the original meaning.

Notice of Medicare Non-Coverage Explanation

Detailed explanation of why current services are no longer covered, and the specific Medicare coverage rules and policy used to make this decision:

The Medicare Benefit Policy Manual, Chapter 8, Section 30 titled "Skilled Nursing Facility Level of Care- General" provided information regarding what care in a skilled nursing facility is covered. We have provided a summary of this information and how it applies to you below.

Medicare guidelines indicate that care in a skilled nursing facility is covered if **all** the following four factors are met:

1. Care your doctor ordered can only be provided by or under the supervision of a nurse or therapist. (See sections 30.2-30.4);
2. You require nursing care on a daily basis or therapy at least 5 days a week (see section 30.6)
3. This care cannot be provided in the home or with the assistance of home health care (see section 30.7)
4. This care must be reasonable and necessary for your specific situation and needs. In addition, the length of the treatment plan and amount of services requested must be reasonable (within a normal limit and not excessive)

If any one of these four factors is not met, continuation of your inpatient skilled nursing services would not be covered, even though it might include the delivery of care that is still needed.

Your care does not have to be provided under the supervision of a nurse or therapist. You do not require nursing care on a daily basis or therapy at least 5 days a week. Your care can be provided in the home or with the assistance of home health care. Therefore, factors one, two, and three are not met.

Now you know.

Let's ask a couple of questions: Why isn't this information readily available? Why must we search for this type of information?

I'm afraid the system is designed for the system and not for everyday citizens of the United States of America.

I call it "profit over people." However, it is time that we consider "people over profit." Who's with me?

What is Congress doing to help its constituents?

In this version, I added quotation marks around "profit over people" and "people over profit" for clarity, and I also corrected "their constituents" to "its constituents" because Congress is a singular entity.

Yet, I still remain faithful, especially if we, the people, would use our voices and vote—not just in a down-ballot way, but in a manner that reflects our research and experiences.

In this version, I added a couple of commas for clarity and to emphasize the "we, the people" phrase. It makes it clearer that you are referring to the collective action of the people.

Faith isn't just about wishful thinking. It's the unwavering belief that, irrespective of the circumstances, God is watching over you.

Faith is placing trust in the hope that someone will step in and advocate for them. This is also where community comes into play, a community of individuals willing to use their voices to stand up for those who need it most.

In what way will you express your faith, especially when faced with a system that you must navigate?

Be Inspired: Make Bold Moves

DEVOTION 33

Be Present

THIS MESSAGE REVOLVES AROUND the thought of how we can support one another. Regardless of the challenges we face, giving up is not an option. We must persevere and discover ways to be there for each other. Prioritizing self-care, both mentally and physically, is essential. Taking care of ourselves empowers us to be fully present for others.

Many of us may be mentally drained and fatigued, especially in today's polarized political climate. It's perfectly fine to rest and recharge, taking the necessary time to rejuvenate our spirits. Although we may feel depleted, it's crucial to continue connecting and sharing our experiences. Engaging with others and staying informed can be taxing, but it's not the end of the road. New voices and leaders are emerging, driven by their prayers and reflections.

We must remain hopeful, resilient, and supportive. Together, we can find ways to be there for one another, to listen, uplift, and show compassion. Let's keep coming together, leaning on each other, and facing these times with strength and unity.

Be Inspired: Make Bold Moves

DEVOTION 34

The Power of Integrity

LET'S LOOK AT THE invaluable quality of integrity, demonstrated by individuals who've acted with remarkable honesty and principle. I believe that most days we have the opportunity to witness people exemplifying unwavering integrity in their actions. This theme of integrity extends to all facets of our lives and prompts us to contemplate its profound significance.

Imagine the transformative impact on the world if we all chose to operate with the utmost integrity, consistently speaking truth to power. The question we must ask ourselves is, "How important is our integrity to us?" Our integrity encompasses qualities like honesty, transparency, and unwavering moral principles, which should guide our words and actions.

Let integrity be the compass for our decisions and interactions. By upholding these values, we contribute to the creation of a fairer and more just world.

Be Inspired: Make Bold Moves

_____
_____
_____
_____
_____
_____
_____
_____
_____
_____
_____
_____
_____
_____
_____
_____
_____
_____
_____
_____
_____
_____
_____
_____
_____
_____
_____
_____
_____
_____

DEVOTION 35

Embracing Change and Transformation

IN THIS UNIQUE SEASON, I firmly believe that God isn't the cause of the circumstances but is using them as an opportunity to draw us closer to Him. It's a time for us to welcome change and transformation into our lives. As our lives adjust and we become more familiar with new ways of fellowship and connection, God encourages us not just to accept these changes but to wholeheartedly embrace and engage with them.

No longer should we reserve expressions of gratitude or acts of kindness for specific occasions. Instead, we should cultivate a lifestyle of compassion, regularly reaching out to others with phone calls, handwritten cards, and love-filled gestures throughout the year.

It's essential to say yes to change and transformation. Take a moment to reflect on what God may be calling you to do differently. Assess your mindset, the condition of your heart, and the areas in need of transformation in your life. Are you open and available for the change that God wants to bring about? This transformation might involve reevaluating things we've taken for granted, such as our desires for gathering in specific places or engaging in particular activities. We must be willing to let go of old patterns and embrace new possibilities.

Rather than clinging to things that might not genuinely enrich our lives, let's actively seek the changes that God encourages us toward. This season may present discomfort and challenges, but it also offers an opportunity for personal growth and a deeper relationship with God. Embrace the stillness, take time to reflect on your life, and remain open to the transformation that God desires to bring about within you.

Be Inspired: Make Bold Moves

DEVOTION 36

Stay In Your Lane

I HAVE ENCOUNTERED MANY individuals who have been discouraged from pursuing what they believe God has called them to do in a particular season. When I ask them about the source of their discouragement, they often mention the opinions and projections of others who suggest they should be doing something else.

I want to remind you not to let other people dictate what you know God has called you to do. Even if there are many others doing similar things, your unique gift and perspective allow you to approach it differently. Don't allow anyone to tell you to abandon your lane and veer off course. Stay focused on what God has called you to do in this season because we need you in that position.

It's important to understand that pursuing something you haven't been called to do can lead to misery. Don't let someone else's perspective or pressure deter you from doing what brings you joy and fulfillment. Recognize your sphere of influence and embrace the fact that we are all different.

Each of us has our own group of people cheering us on, supporting us, and believing in our unique abilities. It's far more fulfilling to be surrounded by a group of people cheering you on than to be influenced by those who doubt your capabilities.

I encourage you to stay true to yourself, your calling, and the path that God has set before you. Don't let the opinions of others deter you from pursuing what brings you fulfillment and aligns with your purpose. Stay in your lane, embrace your uniqueness, and make a positive impact with your gifts.

Be Inspired: Make Bold Moves

DEVOTION 37

Open Our Eyes

I WANT TO ENCOURAGE all of us to open our eyes. There's a powerful passage in Scripture that speaks about removing the scales from our eyes, and my prayer is that God will do just that for each of us. There is a lot happening around us, and it's essential that we take the time to see and understand what's going on. We can't afford to avoid or ignore the important issues that need our attention.

I urge you not to keep putting things on the back burner. It's time to take a stand and be aware of the realities that surround us. One crucial step is to exercise our right to vote and help others do the same. We must be engaged in the democratic process and actively participate in shaping our society.

As I share headlines, causes, and information on *News in Motion*, I encourage you to go beyond just taking my word for it. Take the initiative to verify and fact-check the information for yourself. Use reliable sources and seek different perspectives to gain a well-rounded understanding of the issues at hand. It's through this open-mindedness and informed awareness that we can truly make a difference.

Let us open our eyes, not only to the challenges and problems but also to the opportunities and solutions that lie before us. Let's stay informed, engage in critical thinking, and take meaningful actions to bring about positive change in our world. Together, we can make a difference.

Be Inspired: Make Bold Moves

DEVOTION 38

Resilience and Determination

I WANT TO ENCOURAGE all of us to embrace the spirit of resilience and determination, even though our battles may not be the same as those fought by firefighters risking their lives. We are facing our own fires, challenges, and obstacles that require us to stand firm and fight with everything we have.

In the words of the late John Lewis, let's get into "good trouble" and "necessary trouble." It's time to confront the fires that are approaching us, fueled by adversity and adversity's speed. We must take a stand, rooted in the promises of God and unwavering in our faith. We will not be moved, we will not waver, and we will not give up.

Let us draw inspiration from the story of Hezekiah, who was told by God that he wouldn't have to fight the battle, but he needed to prepare himself for it. Likewise, we have prepared ourselves for this moment, and now it's time to step up and fight. It's time to rally others, to encourage one another, and to be fearless in the face of adversity.

We must remember that the time is now. It's not a time for hesitation or doubt. It's a time to take action, to make our voices heard, and to stand up for what we believe in. Together, we can overcome the challenges that lie before us. Let's fight this fire with determination, faith, and unity.

May we be strengthened by our convictions and guided by the assurance that God is fighting alongside us. With God's support and our collective efforts, we can bring about positive change and emerge victorious. Let us face this battle head-on, knowing that we are not alone and that our fight is just.

Be Inspired: Make Bold Moves

DEVOTION 39

Prayer

I WANT TO REMIND you of the power and importance of prayer. In everything that we do, we should seek guidance and direction from God. Take a moment to pause and ask Him where you need to go, what you need to do, and how you can serve Him and His people. Prayer is a powerful tool that allows us to align our hearts with God's will.

As we navigate through the abundance of news and information around us, I encourage you to verify and research for yourself. Even when watching reputable news stations, take the time to go deeper and understand the laws, rules, and context behind the stories. Seek wisdom and discernment from God as you decipher and make sense of the world around you.

Amidst all the noise and chaos, remember to prioritize self-care. While it's important to raise our voices, protest, and engage in various forms of activism, we must also take time to care for ourselves mentally, emotionally, and spiritually. Create moments of stillness and solitude to be in the presence of God, to pray and connect with Him. In those moments, He will provide clarity, peace, and guidance for the path ahead.

Today and every day, make prayer a priority. Approach God with an open heart, and you will come away with His heart. Seek His wisdom, His direction, and His peace. Through prayer, we can find strength, discernment, and a deeper connection with God as we navigate through the complexities of life.

Be Inspired: Make Bold Moves

_____

_____

_____

_____

_____

_____

_____

_____

_____

_____

_____

_____

_____

_____

_____

_____

_____

_____

_____

_____

_____

_____

_____

_____

_____

_____

_____

DEVOTION 40

Advocacy

ADVOCACY IS A SUBTLE force that floods our daily lives in unexpected ways, often without us realizing it. Remarkably, many of the actions we undertake, both individually and collectively, can be seen as advocacy efforts aimed at championing the rights, interests, and well-being of ourselves or others. Let's look at the diverse realms where advocacy plays a crucial role and discover its enduring impact.

1. Advocacy for Voter Registration. One of the fundamental pillars of a thriving democracy is voter engagement. Advocacy in this context involves encouraging and assisting people in registering to vote. By empowering individuals to exercise their civic duty, advocates contribute to shaping the future of their communities and nations.

2. Advocacy for Senior Care. As our population ages, advocating for seniors to receive the care and support they deserve becomes increasingly important. Advocates work tirelessly to ensure that elderly individuals receive the respect, dignity, and quality of life they have earned through a lifetime of contributions.

3. Advocacy through Education on Social Security. Understanding complex social systems like Social Security can be daunting. Advocates simplify these intricacies by educating others about their rights and benefits, ensuring that individuals can access the resources they need for a secure future.

4. Advocating for Marginalized Communities. In a world that is far from equitable, advocates stand up for those who have been pushed to the fringes. Whether it's fighting against discrimination, unequal opportunities, or systemic biases, they work tirelessly to create a fairer society.

5. Advocacy for Individuals with Disabilities. Championing the rights and dignity of individuals with disabilities is an ongoing mission for many. Advocates seek to remove barriers, promote inclusion, and ensure that everyone, regardless of their abilities, can lead a fulfilling life.

6. Advocating for Strong Marriages. Healthy relationships are the cornerstone of strong families and communities. Advocates support couples by providing resources, counseling, and guidance to navigate the challenges of married life, ultimately strengthening the bonds that hold society together.

7. Advocating for Fair Wages. Economic stability and fairness are vital components of a thriving society. Advocates for higher wages tirelessly campaign for improved working conditions and fair compensation to elevate the quality of life for workers and their families.

8. Advocacy: A Never-Ending Journey. Advocacy is a perpetual journey, an ongoing commitment to making the world a better place. It knows no bounds, and its impact is immeasurable. As individuals and communities, we continue to find new and innovative ways to advocate for ourselves and others, striving for a brighter, more equitable future.

9. Advocating for Social Justice. Social justice lies at the heart of a fair and equitable society. Advocates tirelessly champion the cause of social justice by addressing systemic inequalities, dismantling barriers to opportunities, and fostering inclusivity. They work to ensure that every individual, regardless of their background, can access the same rights, opportunities, and privileges.

10. Advocating for Human Rights. The protection and promotion of human rights is a global imperative. Advocates for human rights are often at the forefront of efforts to combat discrimination, protect freedom of speech, safeguard basic necessities like clean water and education, and hold accountable those who violate fundamental human rights. Their work transcends borders, striving to create a world where every person's dignity and rights are respected and upheld.

Advocacy is not limited to grand gestures or high-profile movements. It thrives in the small, everyday actions we take to empower ourselves and those around us. Whether it's helping someone register to vote, speaking out for the marginalized, or supporting stronger marriages, advocacy is an integral part of the tapestry of our lives. By recognizing its significance and embracing its potential, we can collectively work towards a more just and compassionate world.

Advocacy serves as a powerful force that not only shapes our individual lives but also plays a pivotal role in shaping the future of our communities and the world at large.

Be Inspired: Make Bold Moves

DEVOTION 41

Choose Your Words Carefully

IT IS SO IMPORTANT to speak life into every aspect of our lives. Our words have power, and when we choose to speak life, we are aligning ourselves with the truth and promises of God. Instead of allowing negativity and doubt to consume us, we can intentionally choose to speak words of encouragement, faith, and positivity.

Speaking life goes beyond just affirmations. It's about believing in the potential within us and the work that God has called us to do. It's about declaring blessings, success, and favor over our businesses, careers, and education. When we speak life, we are tapping into the authority and power that God has given us as His children.

At the same time, it's important to be mindful of the words we speak to ourselves and to our circumstances. Let us not cancel out our prayers and positive affirmations with negative self-talk or doubt. Instead, let us consistently speak life and have faith in the transformational power of our words.

In addition to speaking life, we must be informed and take action. It is essential for us to seek knowledge and understanding, to research and vet the information we receive before taking action and sharing it with others. It is crucial to do our research, then empower ourselves and others with accurate information. This is how we can create awareness and drive positive change.

Let us continue to speak life, believe in the greater things that God has called us to, and be diligent in our pursuit of truth and justice. Together, as we uplift and encourage one another, we can make a difference and bring about the transformation we desire to see in our lives and in the world around us.

On *News in Motion*, I encouraged the listeners and viewers to join me in "Watching Our Words." Using the Scripture, "Death and life are in the power of the tongue: and they that love it shall eat the fruit thereof" (Proverbs 18:21, KJV), I encouraged that there should not be any negative talk for thirty days. I asked the viewers and listeners to watch what they spoke and to be mindful of what they received during those thirty days. Perhaps you would like to accept the challenge as you continue reading through *INSPIRE: A Call to Action.*

Be Inspired: Make Bold Moves

DEVOTION 42

We Are the Branches

STOP TRYING TO DO everything on your own. We often fall into the trap of thinking that we need to be self-reliant and handle every task or challenge by ourselves. But the truth is, we were never meant to navigate life alone. God is the vine. We are the branches. It is important to remain in God, and more importantly, we must recognize that asking for help and leaning on others does not make us weak, but rather demonstrates strength and humility.

By reaching out and seeking support from those around us, we can tap into a network of resources, wisdom, and encouragement. We can accomplish so much more when we collaborate, delegate, and rely on the strengths and expertise of others.

Let go of the burden of trying to do it all alone and embrace the power of shared efforts and community. Together, we can achieve great things. Just remember, start with staying connected to God.

> "I am the vine; you are the branches. If you remain in me and I in you, you will bear much fruit; apart from me you can do nothing. If you do not remain in me, you are like a branch that is thrown away and withers; such branches are picked up, thrown into the fire and burned. If you remain in me and my words remain in you, ask whatever you wish, and it will be done for you. This is to my Father's glory, that you bear much

fruit, showing yourselves to be my disciples" (John 15:5-8).

Be Inspired: Make Bold Moves

_____
_____
_____
_____
_____
_____
_____
_____
_____
_____
_____
_____
_____
_____
_____
_____
_____
_____
_____
_____
_____
_____
_____
_____
_____
_____
_____
_____
_____

DEVOTION 43

Be Still and Know

IN THE MIDST OF the chaos and noise of life, it's crucial to find moments of stillness. Be still and know that there is power in silence. Take a pause from the busyness, the worries, and the endless demands. Allow yourself to breathe, to quiet your mind, and to listen. In the stillness, you can connect with your inner self and with something greater than yourself.

It is in these moments of quiet reflection that clarity emerges, peace envelops, and wisdom unfolds. Be still and know that you are not alone on this journey. Trust in the unfolding of life, surrender to the present moment, and find solace in the depths of your own being. Embrace the stillness and let it guide you towards a deeper understanding of yourself and the world around you.

He says, "Be still, and know that I am God; I will be exalted among the nations, I will be exalted in the earth" (Psalm 46:10).

Be Inspired: Make Bold Moves

DEVOTION 44

Keep Pressing

KEEP PRESSING FORWARD TOWARDS the prize, the high calling that awaits you. Don't give up or lose hope in the midst of the news and information overload. Take the time to verify and fact-check what you come across. Be discerning, seeking multiple sources and distinguishing between opinions and facts.

In this journey of life, press towards greater understanding, growth, and truth. Know that speaking truth is a spiritual warfare, and in the pursuit of justice, we engage in this battle. Remain anchored in your faith and trust in God's guidance. Even when doubts or fears arise, surrender them to the flow of Jesus Christ, and continue to vote, to speak truth, and to pursue the truth year after year.

"I press on toward the goal to win the prize for which God has called me heavenward in Christ Jesus" (Philippians 3:14).

Be Inspired: Make Bold Moves

_____
_____
_____
_____
_____
_____
_____
_____
_____
_____
_____
_____
_____
_____
_____
_____
_____
_____
_____
_____
_____
_____
_____
_____

DEVOTION 45

No Weapon Formed

I WANT TO ENCOURAGE you to step boldly into what God has called you to do in this season. Remember that no weapon formed against you shall prosper. Even if you feel like you're under attack or facing obstacles, don't be discouraged. Your unique gifts and talents are needed in this world. Keep pressing forward, trusting in God's guidance and protection.

Stay focused on fulfilling your purpose and making a positive impact. You are an important part of God's plan, and your contributions matter. Embrace your calling and shine your light brightly.

Remember, "No weapon that is formed against thee shall prosper; and every tongue that shall rise against thee in judgment thou shalt condemn. This is the heritage of the servants of the LORD, and their righteousness is of me, saith the LORD" (Isaiah 54:17, KJV).

Be Inspired: Make Bold Moves

_____

_____

_____

_____

_____

_____

_____

_____

_____

_____

_____

_____

_____

_____

_____

_____

_____

_____

_____

_____

_____

_____

_____

_____

_____

_____

_____

_____

_____

DEVOTION 46

Walk It Out

"For we walk by faith, not by sight" (2 Corinthians 5:7, KJV).

I WANT TO REMIND you to walk by faith and not by sight.

It's easy to be overwhelmed by the things we see and hear in the world, but we must hold on to our faith. Despite the challenges and uncertainties, have faith as small as a mustard seed, knowing that God is at work in your life and in the world around you. Trust that He is orchestrating something greater than what we can comprehend. Even when we don't understand the circumstances, choose to respond with faith and hope.

Let your actions and decisions be guided by your unwavering trust in God's plan. Walk boldly in the assurance that He is working all things together for your good. Don't allow fear or doubt to dictate your steps. Instead, hold on to your faith, for it is the key that opens doors, moves mountains, and brings about the miraculous. Keep believing, keep trusting, and keep walking by faith.

Be Inspired: Make Bold Moves

DEVOTION 47

Discover Your "Little Bit of Oil"

HERE'S A DOSE OF inspiration as we embark on our day with a focus on civic engagement and voter education. This inspiration comes from 2 Kings 4, where a woman approached Elisha seeking help. When asked what resources she had, she initially believed she had nothing, except for a small amount of oil.

I encourage all of you to recognize your "little bit of oil." Don't say you have nothing, especially in the context of civic participation. Even if you've faced setbacks like job loss, downsizing, or uncertainty about the future, it's time to ask yourself: "What skills do I possess? What dreams have I yet to pursue? What are my aspirations?"

Just like the woman who had "nothing" but that small amount of oil, your skills and potential are valuable resources. This woman used her tiny bit of oil to pay off her debts and secure her family's future. You can do the same.

Many of us feel like we're at the end of our rope, but remember, even a shoestring can be a lifeline. Use your strengths and capabilities, however limited they may seem, to fulfill your calling in this season of civic engagement and voter participation. The power is within you.

I encourage you to read this passage in 2 Kings 4 for a deeper understanding. Let's harness our collective strength and work towards a better future in civic life. The news starts with you.

Be Inspired: Make Bold Moves

_____

_____

_____

_____

_____

_____

_____

_____

_____

_____

_____

_____

_____

_____

_____

_____

_____

_____

_____

_____

_____

_____

_____

_____

DEVOTION 48

Foolish Arguments

"Stay away from foolish and stupid arguments, because you know they grow into quarrels" (2 Timothy 2:23, NCV).

LET'S DELVE INTO THE realm of unproductive debates. In our lives, we're often faced with situations where disagreements bubble up over various issues, be it politics, gentrification, inflation, or police brutality. These debates, sadly, tend to revolve around minor aspects, leading to unnecessary conflicts and divisions. Rather than diving into these unwise disputes, let's opt for wisdom and insight. We should direct our efforts toward meaningful dialogues, constructive conversations, and genuine attempts to comprehend each other's perspectives.

When the urge to engage in senseless disputes presents itself, it's crucial to recall the value of humility, empathy, and respect. Opt to transcend petty disagreements and embrace a mindset centered on peace and unity. In adopting this approach, we can nurture positive relationships, facilitate personal development, and genuinely influence our world. Thus, let's choose our words wisely, mindfully navigate our interactions, and consciously promote harmony.

Be Inspired: Make Bold Moves

_____

_____

_____

_____

_____

_____

_____

_____

_____

_____

_____

_____

_____

_____

_____

_____

_____

_____

_____

_____

_____

_____

_____

DEVOTION 49

Be Intentional

LET'S COMMIT TO LIVING intentionally. Intentionality is a transformative mindset that can shape your life and the lives of those around you. When you approach each day with intention, you're purposefully harmonizing your actions, thoughts, and words with your goals and values.

Choose to establish clear intentions for your actions and interactions. This means being present and wholeheartedly engaged in each moment, exerting your best effort, and remaining steadfast in your values. It means thoughtfully choosing your words, recognizing their potential to uplift and inspire others.

Intentionality sets in motion a positive ripple effect in the world. Your intentional actions and mindset inspire others to be purposeful as well. Together, we can form a community of purpose-driven individuals, influencing our own lives and the lives of others positively.

As you navigate your day, keep intentionality at the forefront of your mind. Set precise intentions, express gratitude, and conscientiously uphold your values. Embrace each moment as an opportunity to create a constructive influence. By living intentionally, you can craft a life brimming with purpose, happiness, and contentment.

If you haven't registered to vote, be intentional about it and get registered today. Visit www.us.gov. If you are a registered voter, maintain your intentionality by checking your voter registration at least monthly.

Be Inspired: Make Bold Moves

DEVOTION 50

Rejoice and Pray

"Rejoice always, pray continually, give thanks in all circumstances; for this is God's will for you in Christ Jesus" (1 Thessalonians 5:16-18)

REJOICE AND PRAY, FOR these are powerful acts that can transform our hearts and bring us closer to God. Rejoicing is an expression of gratitude and joy in the midst of both triumphs and trials. It is a reminder that even in difficult times, we have reasons to be thankful. By rejoicing, we shift our focus from our worries and challenges to the goodness and faithfulness of God.

Prayer, on the other hand, is our direct line of communication with the Divine. It is a sacred conversation where we can pour out our hearts, seek guidance, and find solace. Through prayer, we invite God into our lives, inviting His wisdom, comfort, and strength to be our companions on the journey. It is through prayer that we align our hearts with God's will and open ourselves to His transformative power.

When we combine rejoicing and prayer, we cultivate a spirit of gratitude and surrender. We rejoice in the blessings we have received and the faithfulness of God, while also surrendering our worries, fears, and desires in prayer. This powerful combination allows us to experience inner peace, find strength in challenging times, and deepen our connection with God.

Let us rejoice and pray without ceasing, for in doing so, we embrace a life of gratitude, trust, and dependence on God. In the highs and lows of life, may we find reasons to rejoice and lift our prayers to the heavens, knowing that God hears us and responds with love and grace.

Be Inspired: Make Bold Moves

DEVOTION 51

Count It All Joy

LET US CONTINUE TO rejoice and give thanks to God for all the blessings He has bestowed upon us. Count it all joy, for every good thing that comes from Him is worthy of our gratitude.

In our moments of prayer and praise, let us express our deep appreciation for God's love, peace, and joy that He fills our hearts with. Let us thank Him for the gift of life, for the breath in our lungs, and for His constant protection and safety amidst challenging times.

As we count it all joy, let us not forget to acknowledge His provision in our finances, His blessings upon our households, and His guidance in our relationships. May we continually offer gratitude for the blessings bestowed upon our marriages and children.

In our celebration of joy, let us come together in a spirit of unity, lifting our voices in praise and thanksgiving. Let us create an atmosphere of joy, where gratitude fills our hearts and spills over into every aspect of our lives.

Count it all joy, and let the joy of the Lord be our strength. Rejoice in His goodness, His faithfulness, and His abundant blessings. Let our hearts overflow with gratitude as we walk this journey of life, knowing that God is with us every step of the way.

"My brethren, count it all joy when you fall into various trials, knowing that the testing of your faith produces patience. But let patience have *its* perfect work, that you may be perfect and complete, lacking nothing. If any of you lacks wisdom, let him ask of God, who gives to all liberally and without reproach, and it will be given to him. But let him ask in faith, with no doubting, for he who doubts is like a wave of the sea driven and tossed by the wind. For let not that man suppose that he will receive anything from the Lord; *he is* a double-minded man, unstable in all his ways" (James 1:2-8, NKJV).

Be Inspired: Make Bold Moves

DEVOTION 52

The Power of Your Vote

YOUR VOTE, YOUR VOICE, holds tremendous power. Its weight is not to be underestimated. It's crucial to engage in thorough research and careful consideration of the candidates on the ballot, evaluating their ethics, values, policies, and the potential repercussions of their election on various aspects of our lives.

Voting is far more than a popularity contest; it's a civic duty that compels us to see the bigger picture. We must scrutinize the candidates' platforms, their track record, and the potential ramifications of their positions on issues such as taxation, business, employment, healthcare, and foreign policy. We must embark on a journey of self-education and enlighten others about the history of voting rights and the significance of being well-informed voters.

Let's refrain from depending on soundbites or advertisements and instead, delve deeper to make informed decisions that align with our values and contribute to the betterment of our society.

The time has come to change the narrative and guarantee that factual information reaches everyone. We must participate in constructive dialogues, promote mutual understanding, and encourage others to conduct their research and play an active role in the democratic process.

Through prayer and informed voting, we can collectively create a significant impact and endeavor towards a brighter future for ourselves and the generations to come.

Be Inspired: Make Bold Moves

DEVOTION 53

Realigning Our Digital Focus

CONSIDER YOUR PRESENCE ON social media. Are you using your platform for positive purposes? Are you harnessing your online presence to highlight local issues and achievements? Is your online activity geared towards uplifting others and showcasing their accomplishments? Reflect on the meaning of being a "follower" and having "followers" in your digital life. The term "following" has a strong presence on social media, drawing attention repeatedly.

Let's turn this contemplation towards a spiritual perspective. Imagine if people followed God throughout their day with the same dedication and interest they give to checking others' social media profiles. How would their lives change if they were as eager to see what God has to say and engage in conversations with the Divine?

This message prompts us to reevaluate our daily habits and priorities. We often invest a considerable amount of time and energy in scrolling through social media, keeping up with others' lives, and engaging in online interactions. However, what if we redirected that same enthusiasm towards connecting with God? What if we eagerly sought divine guidance, wisdom, and messages for our lives?

As we go about our day, amid our social media browsing, God invites us to pause and reflect on what Jesus is communicating. What if we were attentive to the spiritual images, signs, and wonders that God has uniquely designed for us? By shifting our focus and giving our full attention to God, we open ourselves up to a deeper connection with the Divine and the profound impact of His presence.

Therefore, let's be intentional about following Jesus and seeking His guidance throughout our day. Let's prioritize His messages and updates, allowing them to shape our actions, decisions, and interactions. Through this intentionality, we can experience a transformative shift in our lives, gaining a deeper understanding of our purpose and finding fulfillment in walking closely with our Creator.

Be Inspired: Make Bold Moves

DEVOTION 54

Finding Fulfillment in Business and Life

NEVER LOSE WHO YOU are to meet the expectations of others. This message resonates not only in our personal lives but also in the realm of business. It's crucial to remember that staying true to yourself is key to finding fulfillment and success. As a business owner, it's easy to be swayed by the opinions and demands of others, but in doing so, we risk losing our own unique identity and passion.

There may come a point where the weight of external expectations becomes overwhelming, causing us to feel disconnected from our true selves. It's in those moments that we must return to our why—the very foundation that fueled our entrepreneurial journey. Reconnecting with our purpose and the reasons why we started in the first place can reignite our passion and reinvigorate our business.

Taking a much-needed rest break is essential for self-care and rejuvenation. It allows us to step back, recharge, and regain perspective. During this time, we can reflect on our values, passions, and strengths, ensuring that they align with our business endeavors. It is through self-care and introspection that we rediscover our smile and reclaim the joy and excitement that comes from doing what we love.

Let us remember to breathe and embrace the bravery required to stay true to ourselves. Let us prioritize our well-being, listen to our inner voice, and confidently forge our own path. By doing so, we not only find happiness and fulfillment but also inspire others to do the same.

Be Inspired: Make Bold Moves

_____

_____

_____

_____

_____

_____

_____

_____

_____

_____

_____

_____

_____

_____

_____

_____

_____

_____

_____

_____

_____

_____

_____

_____

_____

_____

_____

_____

DEVOTION 55

When the Weight Feels Heavy

DO YOU HAVE A heart burdened for families facing food insecurity, financial struggles, and the overwhelming feeling of being forgotten? I want to convey a message that may be difficult to fully comprehend, but it's important to know that God has not forgotten you. Even in the midst of the hardships and the heavy weight you bear, God is still present.

There have been moments in my own life where I felt abandoned, where I questioned if God truly heard me or if He was by my side. I've experienced times when my joy seemed lost and hope was dim. But as I look back, I can see that God was with me every step of the way. His faithfulness endured, even when my circumstances seemed unbearable.

I understand that my words may not instantly alleviate your struggles or make things easier, but I implore you not to give up. Stay the course and remain faithful, for there is strength in perseverance. In times of uncertainty, hold on to the unwavering belief that God's love and provision are constant. He sees your pain, hears your cries, and walks alongside you.

Seek support from your community, reach out to others who can offer a helping hand, and trust that brighter days will come. Embrace the power of faith and resilience, knowing that God works in ways we may not always understand. Stay rooted in the hope that God's promises endure, and His plans for your life are far greater than the struggles you face.

May you find comfort and renewed strength in knowing that you are not alone. God is with you, holding you close, and guiding you through each step of your journey. Keep pressing forward, and trust that His faithfulness will sustain you.

Be Inspired: Make Bold Moves

_____

_____

_____

_____

_____

_____

_____

_____

_____

_____

_____

_____

_____

_____

_____

_____

_____

_____

_____

_____

_____

_____

_____

_____

_____

_____

_____

_____

_____

_____

DEVOTION 56

Rise Up

"Very truly I tell you, whoever believes in me will do the works I have been doing, and they will do even greater things than these, because I am going to the Father" (John 14:12).

I WANT TO REMIND you of the authority you have as a believer. In John 14:12, it says that we will do even greater things than what Jesus did. As followers of Jesus Christ, we possess the power and authority to make a difference in our world. It's time to access that power and step into the calling that God has placed upon our lives.

We have various means to raise our voices and make an impact. Whether it's through writing to our legislators, utilizing our social media platforms, or speaking up for what is right, we have the ability to bring about positive change. Let go of fear and embrace the love, power, and self-discipline that God has given us.

Remember, fear has no place in our lives. We have been given authority by God, and it's time to exercise it. Take a moment to read John 14:12 and reflect on the power and potential within you. Step into your calling, use your voice, and make a positive impact. Together, we can create a better world and fulfill the greater things that God has called us to do.

Be Inspired: Make Bold Moves

DEVOTION 57

Stick with the Mission

MY INSPIRATIONAL MESSAGE FOR you today is to stick with the mission. In 2 Chronicles 20:15-17, we are reminded that the battle is not ours, but God's. We are called to be fearless and not discouraged, knowing that God is with us. Even if you face challenges or obstacles, remember that you don't have to fight this battle alone.

When it comes to important causes like voter registration, don't be disheartened if not everyone responds. Every single person who registers to vote is a victory. Your efforts matter, and even if you reach just one person, that is a win. Have faith and continue to press forward with your mission.

Remember, you are not alone in this journey. We are all in this together. Let love, power, and a sound mind guide you as you face any challenges that come your way. Trust in God's deliverance and stand firm in your position.

Stay focused on the mission and don't let fear or discouragement deter you. Your dedication and commitment will make a difference. Keep pushing forward, knowing that God is fighting alongside you. Together, we can achieve great things and bring about positive change. Stick to the mission and stay steadfast in your faith.

Be Inspired: Make Bold Moves

DEVOTION 58

Embrace Your Gifts

ARE YOU PASSIONATE ABOUT grassroots organizing, or perhaps you're considering a run for public office? Maybe you excel in fundraising, campaign management, or connecting with people on a personal level. Are you a gifted writer? Whatever your strengths and talents may be, it's time to harness them for positive change.

If you feel called to be a catalyst for change, don't hesitate. Step forward and become a vocal advocate for the causes you're passionate about. If your gift lies in connecting with others, pick up the phone and engage in heartfelt conversations. Unlike easily overlooked text messages, personal calls have the power to leave a lasting impression.

Start with your foundation, your family, and friends. This week, I urge you to take on a task: email your loved ones and share why voting matters to you. Open up and reveal your personal experiences and beliefs. By doing so, you can inspire and motivate others to participate in the democratic process.

Never forget that each of us possesses the ability to influence those in our circles. By embracing your unique talents and sharing your fervor, you can ignite change and create a ripple effect of engagement and awareness. Be true to yourself, utilize your gifts, and ensure your voice is heard. Together, we can forge a society where every voice holds significance and every vote makes an impact.

Be Inspired: Make Bold Moves

_____

_____

_____

_____

_____

_____

_____

_____

_____

_____

_____

_____

_____

_____

_____

_____

_____

_____

_____

_____

_____

_____

_____

_____

_____

_____

_____

_____

_____

_____

_____

DEVOTION 59

Raise the Question

RAISE THE QUESTION, "WHO told you that?" This simple yet powerful inquiry can help us navigate through the abundance of information and opinions we encounter. When faced with questionable information, it is crucial to research the content and verify the source. If something doesn't sound right, it's likely not right. We must be diligent in seeking reliable sources and separating fact from fiction.

In today's digital age, misinformation and manipulated images can easily circulate. It is essential to scrutinize the content we come across, especially on social media platforms. Take for example a doctored photo found on the internet or on social media. By raising the question, "Who told you that?" and conducting thorough research, we can uncover the truth behind such images. In this case, the doctored photo was designed to mislead, and recognizing it allows us to discern fact from fiction.

Similarly, raising the question applies to the opinions and doubts others may project onto us. When someone tells you that you cannot succeed or that you cannot make a difference in getting people to register to vote, challenge their perspective. Ask, "Who told you that?" and evaluate the basis of their claims. Often, negative beliefs or limiting narratives stem from misconceptions or personal biases. By questioning these assertions, we empower ourselves to challenge the status quo and prove them wrong.

Let us be diligent in our research, critical in our analysis, and courageous in raising the question, "Who told you that?" Embrace a mindset of seeking truth, rejecting misinformation, and challenging limiting beliefs. Through this process, we can navigate the vast sea of information and make informed decisions that align with our values and aspirations.

Be Inspired: Make Bold Moves

DEVOTION 60

Engage. Reflect. Connect.

"pray continually" (1 Thessalonians 5:17).

ENGAGE WITH THE WORDS on the page, not just as mere text, but as a source of wisdom and guidance. Reflect on these words, allowing them to penetrate your thoughts and transform your perspective. Then, in prayer, find stillness, acknowledging the presence of a God who embodies justice, forgiveness, and understanding.

Make a deliberate choice to read with understanding, meditate to internalize and grow, and pray with the assurance that God's strength will empower you to stand unwaveringly, even in the face of life's challenges.

Be Inspired: Make Bold Moves

DEVOTION 61

Unshakable Power Over Fear

"The LORD is with me; I will not be afraid. What can mere mortals do to me?" (Psalm 118:6).

PSALM 118:6 REMINDS US of an unassailable truth: nothing and no one holds dominion over us. Let's awaken to our inherent power to live victoriously, casting aside fear's chains. It's time to fully embrace the certainty that God is our ally, dismantling fear's hold on us.

Don't shy away from what you might consider challenging conversations. People often steer clear of discussions that could lead to conflicts. However, I want to propose today that you can overcome fear with unwavering courage. Don't let fear dictate your actions.

Anchor your trust in the Lord wholeheartedly. His unwavering truth and promises will dissolve fear's grasp. When you ponder Psalm 118:6, let it echo within you: "The LORD is with me; I will not be afraid. What can mere mortals do to me?" This declaration is your shield against fear, a reminder of your unshakable strength in God's embrace.

Be Inspired: Make Bold Moves

DEVOTION 62

Embrace Stillness and Await

"For God alone, O my soul, wait in silence, for my hope is from him. He only is my rock and my salvation, my fortress; I shall not be shaken" (Psalm 62:5-6, ESV).

IN LIFE'S JOURNEY, THERE come moments when silence is our path. We often rush to vocalize the divine whispers that grace our ears. I've known that impulse. I hear God's voice, and too quickly I'm sharing it, especially with the person it was intended for. Yet, there are times when God calls us to silence, to prayer, rather than speech. Frequently, God unveils insights for us to hold in prayer, not to voice aloud. Sometimes God beckons us to glimpse the path He lays before us, not to tread it alone but to clasp His hand in unison. In the hush of silence, await with expectation.

Be Inspired: Make Bold Moves

DEVOTION 63

Empowerment Message and Call to Pray

WHILE PENNING *INSPIRE*, I felt a powerful surge of determination and purpose course through me. Deep within, I held an unwavering belief that something truly extraordinary is on the horizon.

Although I may not fully comprehend the divine inspiration that urged me to write this devotional, I ponder the impact it will have on the lives of others. At this very moment, as I write these words, I sense that people will be stirred to become more involved in their communities and engage in civic matters. This is an empowerment to participate actively.

As a collective, let's unite our hands and hearts in prayer. Our fervent prayers should target not only the absence of material resources but also the spiritual lack in our lives. Together, let's visualize abundance, doors of opportunity, and blessings cascading abundantly into our lives and the lives of those around us. In unison, let's work on eradicating jealousy and envy from our hearts, recognizing that these emotions hinder our progress. In their stead, let's celebrate each other's victories, nurture one another's dreams, and cheer for each other. In essence, let's build a community.

While crafting this book, I reached out to intercessors who understand the potent impact of our collective prayers. Each of you who joins this cause becomes a beacon of light, something that doesn't sit well with those who oppose us.

Whether we've touched the life of one person or many, we've made an impact, and that's certainly something to celebrate.

Let's embark on this journey of bold prayer together. Let's make declarations and decrees against lack in the name of Jesus. Let's proclaim an immediate release of resources, healing for the sick, protection for every household, reconciliation in marriages, and strengthened family bonds. We'll pray for the eradication of food insecurity, especially for those who are marginalized, the safeguarding of election poll workers, the integrity of electoral processes, and the triumph of truth.

For those grappling with financial challenges, whether it's foreclosure, rent, or debt, we shall decree favor and cancellation, trusting in the miraculous turnarounds that Jesus can orchestrate.

Always remember, the core of our message revolves around a man named Jesus. His resurrection embodies power, access, and authority for all of us. As He promised, we can accomplish even greater things than He did. That power resides within you, so refrain from waiting for external assistance, and acknowledge the strength that dwells within.

May this message infuse you with hope, confidence, and the unwavering belief that greatness is within your grasp. Carry this energy with you and let's keep moving forward in faith and unity.

Be Inspired: Make Bold Moves

_____
_____
_____
_____
_____
_____
_____
_____
_____
_____
_____
_____
_____
_____
_____
_____
_____
_____
_____
_____
_____
_____
_____
_____
_____

DEVOTION 64

United Prayer for a Hopeful Future

TODAY'S DEVOTIONAL HOLDS A special place in my heart. It's a message about the profound power of prayer, echoing the scriptural wisdom that "the prayers of the righteous avail much." Now, more than ever, it's crucial that we unite in prayer, regardless of the election's outcome. The truth is, we're stepping into the unknown after this election. We can't predict people's reactions or anticipate the challenges that may lie ahead. That's precisely why I want to stress the importance of shrouding our nation, its leaders, and ourselves in prayer.

It's time to saturate the world with prayer. Let's invest time praying for every candidate, irrespective of our differences. Let our prayers extend to all elected officials, national guards, local police, government employees at all levels, teachers, social workers, and every individual who contributes to the fabric of our society. But our efforts should not stop there—let's also enfold our individual households in prayer.

Recall, "the prayers of the righteous avail much." We are at a pivotal moment, and our prayers possess the potential to create a profound impact. Just as people have been urging us to vote because our lives depend on it, I want to emphasize that our prayers are equally vital. Our lives depend on them too.

Take a moment to look around. What do you see? What can you discern? Take these observations and commit them to prayer. In a world where people are grappling with overwhelming challenges, prayer is essential. Hunger persists, families are disintegrating, democracy faces threats, and misinformation and disinformation are rampant on social media. Our prayers can serve as a guiding light in these troubled times.

Be Inspired: Make Bold Moves

DEVOTION 65

Transform Assumptions

GOD'S ACCEPTANCE OR REJECTION of a person is not based on their race, nationality, or cultural identity. So why do we find it necessary to pass judgment on others due to these differences, whether subtly or overtly? Social scientists describe culture as the underlying values, standards, and expectations that shape human interactions. It encompasses etiquette, preferences, language, traditions, food, clothing, musical tastes, and belief systems. Just as culture influences our worldview and behavior, it also influences how we interpret the actions of others.

Our learned behaviors, biases, fears, and stereotypes can often hinder healthy communication and trust. However, since these behaviors are learned, they can also be unlearned. Our unique experiences and cultural backgrounds shape our reactions, perceptions, and thought processes. What we perceive as reality and what we disregard is largely determined by our experiences and cultural influences. Due to differing assumptions and perceptions, we sometimes fail to see what exists and imagine what doesn't. Changing our assumptions and perceptions is vital in the process of choosing what to believe.

Be Inspired: Make Bold Moves

DEVOTION 66

Register to Vote, America

TAKE A VITAL STEP today by registering to vote. It's a simple process, and your voice truly matters. Visit one of the following links to register:

www.USA.gov
www.Vote.org
www.Vote.gov
www.rockthevote.org
www.whenweallvote.org
www.iwillvote.com

But don't stop there; consider becoming a poll worker. Your efforts can help ensure that all polling locations remain open, particularly in marginalized areas. Visit www.PowerThePolls.com/NewsInMotion to get involved.

Remember, every voice counts, and every vote makes a difference. Your participation shapes the future.

Be Inspired: Make Bold Moves

DEVOTION 67

You Got This

AMIDST THE CHALLENGES AND obstacles that surround us, let's take a moment to draw inspiration from the Bible's stories. Think about those in history who faced oppression and how God assured them of victory.

Reflect on the New Testament, where Jesus' presence brought hope. In my own words, as I delve into these Scriptures, I hear Jesus saying, "Look, My child, you've got this. Trust Me, even in adversity, you've got this." So I share the same message with all of you: You've got this.

Though weariness and challenges may try to break through, remember that inside you, there's unwavering strength. While difficulties might seem daunting, have confidence, for you possess the resilience to conquer them. We've got this, my friends. We truly do.

Let's take action and keep moving forward.

Be Inspired: Make Bold Moves

DEVOTION 68

Assisted Living: A Call to Action

NURSING HOMES IN THE United States receive a substantial $100 billion annually from American taxpayers. Yet, it's disheartening to note that many facilities remain understaffed, leading to concerns about the quality of care provided. As responsible citizens who diligently contribute our taxes, it's imperative for us to act and be advocates for our loved ones, family members, and friends who may find themselves in substandard living conditions. Furthermore, addressing issues such as avoidable injuries, inadequate regulation, and underpaid staff is equally important. In this blog post, we've compiled ways to advocate for improved nursing home care and to ensure that our hard-earned tax dollars are utilized effectively.

1. **Stay Informed.** One of the initial steps in advocating for better nursing home care is to stay informed about the current state of the industry. Conduct research and gather data about nursing home facilities in your area, assess their staffing levels, and investigate any reported incidents of neglect or abuse. Knowledge is a powerful tool, and being informed empowers you to take effective action.

2. **Connect with Advocacy Groups.** Numerous advocacy organizations are dedicated to nursing home reform and the rights of residents. Joining these groups can provide you with valuable resources,

support, and a platform to voice your concerns. Organizations like AARP, the National Consumer Voice for Quality Long-Term Care, and local senior advocacy groups offer excellent starting points.

3. **Engage with Elected Officials.** As taxpayers and voters, we have the right to express our concerns to elected officials. Reach out to your local, state, and federal representatives to articulate your apprehensions about nursing home care in your community. Advocate for stronger regulations, increased funding for oversight, and policies that prioritize the well-being of nursing home residents.

4. **Attend Public Meetings.** Many issues related to nursing homes are discussed in public meetings and hearings. Attend these events to ensure your voice is heard. Share your personal experiences or concerns, and motivate others to do the same. Public pressure can be instrumental in bringing about positive changes.

5. **Support Whistleblowers.** Employees of nursing homes who witness neglect or abuse often fear retaliation when they speak out. Offer your support to whistleblowers and advocate for laws that protect them from retribution. Encourage employees to report incidents and violations, as their insights can be indispensable for enhancing care.

6. **Raise Awareness.** Utilize social media, community events, and local media outlets to raise awareness about nursing home care issues. Share stories, statistics, and personal experiences to educate others and garner public support for reform.

7. **Monitor Nursing Home Ratings.** Federal and state agencies provide ratings and inspection reports for

nursing homes. Regularly check these ratings to identify facilities that may be struggling with the quality of care. Share this information with your community to facilitate informed decision-making.

As concerned citizens and taxpayers, it is our duty to advocate for improved nursing home care. By staying informed, connecting with advocacy groups, engaging with elected officials, attending public meetings, supporting whistleblowers, raising awareness, and monitoring nursing home ratings, we can collectively work towards ensuring that our loved ones and fellow community members receive the care and dignity they rightfully deserve. It's time to take action and hold nursing homes accountable for the $100 billion they receive annually from American taxpayers.

Be Inspired: Make Bold Moves

DEVOTION 69

Truth. Integrity. Reputation.

HAVE WE LOST TRUTH, integrity, and reputation? It is so important to carry these three, especially when running for an elected office, serving as an advocate, or simply living your life as an everyday citizen. Yet, for some, such as advocates and politicians, these principles hold an even greater significance. Your roles carry the weight of public trust and responsibility. The decisions you make, the policies you advocate for, and the conduct you display directly impact the lives of countless individuals and the state of our society.

Advocates, your dedication to truth, integrity, and a sterling reputation is not only admirable but essential. In your pursuit of justice and social change, the very essence of your work hinges on credibility. By living out these values, you inspire trust and rally others to your causes.

Politicians, the importance of these principles cannot be overstated. The decisions you make shape the course of nations. The choices you champion affect the livelihoods of entire populations. Upholding the ideals of truth, integrity, and a distinguished reputation isn't just a personal endeavor; it's a public duty.

The integrity we all embody influences the perception of institutions, governments, and the very essence of democracy. It is not just a call to live in truth, integrity, and reputation; it's a solemn obligation to be the guardians of these principles in the public sphere.

In a world rife with misinformation and skepticism, your unwavering commitment to these principles acts as a beacon, lighting the path towards a more just and virtuous society. May your advocacy and political careers forever stand as a testament to the transformative power of truth and integrity.

What say you?

Be Inspired: Make Bold Moves

DEVOTION 70

Dreams

PURSUING YOUR DREAMS WITH passion and unwavering perseverance is a journey marked by God's unique design for each of us. Within our dreams and aspirations lie the purpose that drives us in this world.

It's imperative to recognize that even in the face of doubt or ridicule from others, those dreams hold a sacred place within us. God has instilled these desires for a divine reason. Our pursuit of them isn't about seeking recognition or boasting but a testament to God's goodness and faithfulness in our lives.

In this pursuit, we must not forget the strength of community and the power of connection. Building relationships isn't just about personal gain but sharing our resources, knowledge, and opportunities. It's through unity that we can achieve far more than we ever could in isolation.

For those drawn to politics and leadership, it's paramount that we support and empower those who aspire to make a difference. If your passion lies in politics or community service, reach out and connect with like-minded individuals who share your vision. Seek mentorship from experienced figures in the field, and don't shy away from actively participating in the process of change.

In addition, let's not lose sight of the broader perspective. Despite our differences in policies and beliefs, we must come together, united in purpose. Strengthening our union requires collaboration, finding common ground, and pursuing shared objectives. It's through unity that we can bring about substantial change and shape a brighter future for everyone.

Lastly, embrace constructive criticism and encircle yourself with diverse perspectives. Personal growth and development emerge when we are open to listening, learning, and challenging our own convictions. Like iron sharpening iron, engaging in respectful and considerate dialogue refines our ideas and equips us to navigate life's complexities effectively.

Dare to dream big, foster connections with others, and wholeheartedly embrace the path that lies ahead. Together, as a supportive community, let us each play our unique roles, working collaboratively to leave an enduring impact on the world that surrounds us.

Be Inspired: Make Bold Moves

DEVOTION 71

Unique

THERE IS A BEAUTIFUL truth found in Psalm 139 that we are uniquely and wonderfully made. Each one of us has a purpose and a calling that is special and significant. Whether we are warriors, prayer warriors, peacemakers, or seekers of stillness, we are all uniquely made to fulfill our individual roles in this world.

As we journey in our unique calling, it is important for us to stay rooted in God's Word and seek His guidance and strength. The Word of God provides us with wisdom, encouragement, and direction. It is through His Word that we find the strength to navigate the challenges and intensities of life.

Secure a prayer partner and commit to cover one another in prayer, seeking divine protection, guidance, and strength for the journey ahead. Let us not walk this path alone but come together in unity, supporting and interceding for one another.

While we anticipate that the days, months, or years ahead may intensify, we should not be filled with fear but with preparedness and wisdom. We need to stay the course, remaining vigilant and watchful, ready to navigate any challenges that may arise. Having a plan, being mindful of our surroundings, and seeking God's guidance in all we do will help us walk this journey with wisdom and discernment.

Let us not be discouraged or fearful, but let us embrace the journey ahead with faith, courage, and the assurance that God is with us. We are uniquely made, called, and equipped for such a time as this. May we continue to seek God's guidance, support one another, and stay rooted in His Word as we fulfill our purpose in this world.

Stay strong, stay focused, and stay connected to the Source of our strength. God is with us, and together, we can overcome any challenge that comes our way.

Be Inspired: Make Bold Moves

_____
_____
_____
_____
_____
_____
_____
_____
_____
_____
_____
_____
_____
_____
_____
_____
_____
_____
_____
_____
_____
_____
_____
_____
_____

DEVOTION 72

Power. Love. Sound Mind.

"For God hath not given us the spirit of fear; but of power, and of love, and of a sound mind" (2 Timothy 1:7, KJV).

HERE'S A REMINDER THAT God has not given us a spirit of fear, but of power, love, and a sound mind. It's important for us to embrace this truth and not allow fear to control our actions or hinder our progress.

With the power that God has given us, we can stand up for what is right, speak out against injustice, and make a positive impact in the world. Love is a powerful force that can bring about transformation and unity, and we should strive to love both our neighbors and ourselves.

Operating in a sound mind means making decisions based on wisdom and discernment. It's crucial to educate ourselves, research, and seek understanding before making choices, including when it comes to voting. By aligning our actions with the principles of love, justice, and equality, we can contribute to a better society for all.

Jesus demonstrated love and compassion for all people, regardless of their background or circumstances. He showed us the importance of caring for the marginalized and the vulnerable, and we can follow in His footsteps by extending love and support to those in need.

Let us move forward with confidence, knowing that we have the power, love, and sound mind to make a positive difference in the world. May we continue to walk in faith, love, and wisdom, guided by the principles of the Word.

Stay strong, and may you be filled with courage, compassion, and a clear mind as you navigate through this season.

May I pray for you? If so,

God, in the name of Jesus, deliver us from fear. Remind Your children that You have given us power, love, and a sound mind. You have given us self-control. Lord, help us tap into this truth and live our lives accordingly. Thank You for Your grace and mercy and for the power to stand in the full armor of God. Lord, we accept that You have given us the authority to do greater things, as You state in John 14:12. Amen.

Be Inspired: Make Bold Moves

DEVOTION 73

Thankful

GRATITUDE IS ESSENTIAL. IT'S crucial to remain attuned to the sensitivities and challenges that individuals may be wrestling with, especially in the aftermath of events such as a debate, which can stir intense emotions and resurrect painful memories for some.

By reaching out and extending words of encouragement, prayers, and a supportive presence, we have the power to create a positive influence in the lives of those enduring tough times. Your compassion and your readiness to listen and stand by others showcase the might of empathy and human connection.

Many among us may have weathered trauma, abuse, or challenging childhoods, and their journey towards healing is ongoing. Through our care and support, we can offer them a comforting embrace, strength, and the assurance that they are not alone.

Consider taking a moment to gaze at a picturesque window display or embark on a delightful road trip for a well-deserved break. Providing yourself with the space to rest and rejuvenate is vital for sustaining your well-being and resilience. Seize this opportunity to unwind and recharge.

I thank God for your unwavering dedication and commitment to the path that unfolds before you.

I pray that your endeavors in doing good for others, raising awareness, and mobilizing for constructive change are producing a tangible impact. Keep forging ahead, and may your journey be adorned with blessings and a revitalized vigor.

Remember, self-care is important. Therefore, take good care, and always remember that you are valued for the profound influence you bring to the lives of those around you.

I am thankful for you!

Be Inspired: Make Bold Moves

_____
_____
_____
_____
_____
_____
_____
_____
_____
_____
_____
_____
_____
_____
_____
_____
_____
_____
_____
_____
_____
_____
_____
_____
_____
_____
_____

DEVOTION 74

Navigating Stress and Impact

LET'S DEDICATE SOME TIME to underscore the significance of self-care and proactive measures when faced with stress and uncertainties. Prioritizing our well-being, encompassing both physical and mental health, is of paramount importance, particularly during testing periods. When we confront the hurdles and hardships in our path, they can be overwhelming, inducing stress and anxiety. However, there are steps we can take to address these challenges while ensuring our self-care.

Above all, prayer stands as a significant tool, offering comfort, tranquility, and guidance. Turning to God in prayer enables us to release our burdens and apprehensions to Him, relying on His wisdom and provision. Through prayer, we can discover resilience, clarity, and a sense of serenity that transcends understanding.

Furthermore, practical action is essential. Encouraging and motivating others to participate in the electoral process is a meaningful stride in fostering positive change within our communities and the nation. Your commitment to arranging webinars and sharing mobilization resources is commendable. By disseminating information, memes, and strategies for engaging others through social media, you empower individuals to take action and ensure their voices are heard in the democratic sphere.

Nonetheless, self-care should not be overlooked amidst our endeavors to effect change. Prioritizing our physical and emotional well-being is essential. This may encompass setting boundaries, practicing relaxation techniques, partaking in activities that bring joy, seeking support from loved ones, and ensuring we receive sufficient rest and nourishment.

It's vital to remember that self-care is not a selfish act, but instead a foundational necessity for us to effectively and sustainably impact the world around us. By tending to our own well-being, we can better serve others and display greater resilience when confronting challenges.

I believe we have a responsibility to inspire others to vote, educate and mobilize, and advocate for positive transformations. Yet, do not forget to reserve moments for yourself, to seek solace and strength in prayer, and to engage in self-care as you journey forward.

May God bestow upon you the wisdom, endurance, and grace to navigate stress and uncertainties while making an enduring impact in the lives of others.

Be Inspired: Make Bold Moves

DEVOTION 75

Stay the Course

AS I SHARE IN all of my books, "staying the course is crucial in any endeavor, including our journey of faith and the pursuit of our goals." The call to press towards the prize of the high calling reminds us to stay focused, determined, and unwavering in our pursuit of righteousness and God's purposes for our lives.

In these challenging times, it is easy to become weary and discouraged, especially when faced with the difficulties and uncertainties of the world around us. But we are called to rise above weariness and stay committed to the course set before us. Just like athletes who train and push themselves to reach the finish line, we too must press on with endurance, relying on God's strength and guidance.

As believers, we have the assurance that God is with us every step of the way. He empowers us, sustains us, and provides the strength we need to overcome obstacles and stay the course. It is through prayer, studying God's Word, and seeking His guidance that we find the inspiration, wisdom, and determination to continue pressing forward.

Put on your game face as a powerful reminder to prepare yourself mentally, spiritually, and emotionally for the challenges ahead. Just as athletes focus and gear up before a competition, we need to tap into our inner strength and rely on the power of the Holy Spirit within us.

Actively participating in the democratic process and encouraging others to do the same, we can collectively contribute to positive change in our communities and nation.

Let us stay the course. Let us remain steadfast in our faith, resolute in our pursuit of righteousness, and committed to making a difference. With God's strength, guidance, and grace, we can press on towards the prize, knowing that our efforts and perseverance are not in vain.

May God bless you abundantly as you continue to stay the course and make a lasting impact in the world around you.

Be Inspired: Make Bold Moves

_____

_____

_____

_____

_____

_____

_____

_____

_____

_____

_____

_____

_____

_____

_____

_____

_____

_____

_____

_____

_____

_____

_____

_____

_____

_____

DEVOTION 76

Ask Questions

AS ADVOCATES FOR OUR loved ones, we must learn to ask the necessary questions. After her recent hospital bouts, I glanced at my mom's nightstand in her room and was floored by the number of prescription bottles. I couldn't help but wonder if different prescriptions were counteracting any others.

I started asking questions to myself and my mom. Is food necessary to take this pill? Should this medication be taken on an empty stomach? What are the side effects of this prescription? Can the medications be taken together? So many questions for which I did not have answers. Luckily for us, I know someone in medicine who can help decipher the different prescriptions and help my mom keep track of things. But not everyone has that on their side. So how do you advocate for yourself and your loved ones?

At the time of writing this book, we have been on the air with *News in Motion* for more than three years. It was after one of the episodes when I received a number of questions about advocating for your health and well-being. I decided to write an article in one of my eNewsletters, which I share in today's inspirational message, as follows.

First, you must be your primary advocate for your health and well-being. If advocating for yourself isn't possible, bring someone along with you to your appointments who will. Transparent moment: I have a condition called Lymphomatoid papulosis. When I was first diagnosed, all I heard was the word cancer. I missed everything the doctor said afterward because I was trying to hold it together. I was admitted that day because, at that time, it was considered a rare condition, especially for a person of color. Thank God my sister was there who could explain to me what the doctor said. She was the one who asked question after question to help gather all the information we needed so that I could continue my journey of life. Therefore, it is just as important to serve as the advocate of a loved one who may not be able to advocate for themselves.

Have you ever left the doctor's office, urgent care, or the hospital with any of the following?

- You are unsure about your doctor's terms, phrases, or language.
- You are unclear about the diagnosis.
- You were given instructions but did not fully comprehend how to take prescribed medication or care for yourself with the diagnosis you received.
- You are unsure if you have explained yourself well and your symptoms to your nurse or doctor.
- You are unclear about what's next after your appointment.

Don't worry. Most of us have been there a time or two.

QUESTIONS TO CONSIDER AND ASK FOR ANY MEDICAL SITUATION:

1. In layman's terms, what is going on with me? What's going on with my loved one?

Yes, ask the doctor to explain what is going on with you. If you still don't understand, keep asking until you do. Have the confidence to ask your doctor to explain what's happening inside your body in non-medical terms that you can understand.

Ask follow-up questions to gain a clearer understanding.

- How serious is the condition?
- Is there anything you need to do immediately?
- How will this condition impact your everyday life?
- Is this a chronic condition?
- How soon will you begin to see things get better?
- Will this condition worsen?
- Is this something that will take care of itself over time?
- What caused this to happen?
- Is this condition contagious?

Do not be afraid to ask questions, and do not respond in fear. I know fear can take over sometimes, but remember, "God did not give us a spirit of fear."

2. How should I care for myself? How should I care for my loved one?

After I was able to push past hearing the word cancer, I learned I have a chronic papulonecrotic skin disease with histologic features suggestive of malignant lymphoma. When I break out due to eating the wrong things, being exposed to dust, and or too much stress in my life, the bumps take up to two months to heal, usually leaving slightly depressed oval scars. Therefore, with my condition of Lymphomatoid papulosis, I needed to know how to care for my new skin condition. I love the sun. I love pineapples. I love swimming. I hate dusting. I needed to know, "Now what?"

A ton of information is shared during emergency hospital visits and regular doctor appointments regarding the condition, your treatment, self-care, and so forth. It is essential to understand all discharge and other instructions. Therefore, it is critical to understand any medication that has been prescribed.

- What are the side effects?
- Are there any interactions? (Bring a written list of your medications, supplements, and vitamins to *every* appointment.)
- How do I take it?
- Do I take it on an empty stomach? With food?
- How long do I need to take it?
- How much will it cost? Can I use GoodRx?
- Does insurance cover it?
- Is a generic or any other name brand than what is prescribed okay?
- Are there any alternative treatments?
- How will it affect my mind?
- How will I feel?
- Can I drive?
- Will I have to take this medication for the remainder of my life?
- Will my body get accustomed to this prescription?
- What happens if I do not finish taking the prescribed medication?
- What if I decide not to take the medication?

There are times when a physician will order tests to confirm a diagnosis. Do not simply say, "Okay." Ask questions for yourself or your loved ones.

- Why did you schedule this particular test?
- What do you hope to find or rule out from this test?
- Are there risks/side effects to taking these tests?

- What is the time frame for taking this test?
- When and how will I get the results?
- What happens after I get the results?

3. Why?

Never be afraid or intimidated to ask why. Not sure why your doctor wants to place you on a particular prescription? Not sure why you need a CT scan? An MRI? Ask why. There's a change in your medication? Ask the question. Ask why.

4. What should I expect?

If you're undergoing surgery or having treatment, you should understand approximately how long it will take and know all post-op information. You should also know if you need a driver or someone to accompany you. If you're waiting on test results, you should know when you can expect to hear back.

5. Ask about follow-up.

You need to know what's next. Follow up with which doctor? When should you schedule your next appointment?

NOTEBOOKS ARE KEY

Yes, I am the notebook queen. I have a notebook for everything. I take a three-ring binder with me to my appointments. I have tabs for each doctor and place for reports, lab work, questions, and all my supplements, vitamins, and medicines, and I will hand copies to the nurse and the doctor for their records.

5. Don't be afraid to report negative interactions.

Most hospitals have a patient advocacy office. Their role is to assist in providing a voice for patients as needed (especially if you need an advocate and are unable to bring your own) and as a way to have accountability for staff and ensure the best patient care is being provided. Use that notebook I mentioned, note any negative or uncomfortable interactions, and report those to the Patient Advocacy Office. Your voice and your experience need to be heard.

Whatever you do, ask questions. This list helps you become your own advocate and an advocate for your loved ones.

Now that you have the necessary list, please use it during your future appointments and share the list with your loved ones.

Be Inspired: Make Bold Moves

DEVOTION 77

We Can

"I can do all things through Christ who strengthens me" (Philippians 4:13, NKJV).

PHILIPPIANS 4:13, A STEADFAST reminder that through Christ's empowerment, our potential knows no bounds. As we tread this journey, let's cherish the fact that we're not solitary travelers but a community of faithful souls, summoned to stand together, bolster one another, and enact a transformative influence on the world. When we converge in Christ's name, our combined endeavors harbor the promise of profound change.

Within each of us resides an exclusive mixture of gifts, talents, and passions. As we channel these endowments and allow the divine to flow through us, we metamorphose into instruments of His boundless love, grace, and might. We hold the power to infuse hope into despairing hearts, mend the broken, and illuminate the darkest corners of existence.

Find solace in the awareness that the fortitude and vigor of Christ pulse within us. Let's embrace our divine calling and step out with unwavering faith to shape the destiny of our families, communities, and the world. United, we can extend mutual support and resilience.

Let's unite in prayer, beseeching for strength and valor. Rely on the determined vigor supplied by Christ, and advance audaciously on the path He has laid before us. Inspire one another, commemorate each other's victories, and provide unwavering backing in the face of adversity.

Bear in mind, with Christ as our companion, we are capable of achieving remarkable feats. Go forth with unwavering faith, cognizant that our combined toil can bring about profound transformation, all while magnifying His glory. Together, we can make an indelible mark and touch lives for His eternal Kingdom.

Take courage and draw inspiration, for you are furnished and emboldened by the might of Christ. Let's march ahead, confident in the knowledge that "we can," and in doing so, let's build vibrant communities, facilitate voter registration, extend love to our neighbors, champion others, feed the hungry, and embrace the unity that binds us all.

Be Inspired: Make Bold Moves

DEVOTION 78

Prayer Community

I WANT TO EMPHASIZE the power of prayer. Prayer is a divine connection that brings us closer to God and allows us to seek His guidance, comfort, and intervention. In times of uncertainty, turmoil, and challenges, it is through prayer that we find solace and strength.

As believers, we are called to pray fervently and persistently. Yes, "pray without ceasing" (1 Thessalonians 5:17, ESV). The Bible reminds us that the prayers of the righteous have great impact. When we come before God with humility, faith, and sincerity, our prayers become a powerful force that can bring about transformation in our lives and the world around us.

Let us not underestimate the significance of prayer, especially during this crucial time of elections and decision-making. Prayer has the ability to shape outcomes, soften hearts, and bring about justice and righteousness. Through prayer, we can intercede for our communities, our leaders, and those in need. We can pray for wisdom, unity, and the manifestation of God's will in our lives and in the world.

In addition to personal prayer, let us also join together in corporate prayer. Praying with others amplifies our petitions and strengthens our faith. It creates a sense of unity and community, reminding us that we are not alone in our journey.

I encourage you to make prayer a priority in your life. Take time each day to connect with God, to pour out your heart, and to listen for His guidance. Pray for discernment, clarity, and the courage to stand for what is right. Pray for the well-being of your loved ones, your community, and the world at large. Pray for wisdom and compassion to guide your actions.

Know that your prayers make a difference. They have the power to bring about transformation, healing, and restoration. Trust in God's faithfulness and believe that He hears your prayers. Even when the outcome is not immediate or as expected, continue to pray with faith and perseverance, knowing that God is working in ways beyond our understanding.

Let us be a people of prayer, united in seeking God's will and walking in His ways. As we pray, may we experience His peace, His guidance, and His presence in our lives. May our prayers bring about positive change and be a source of hope and strength for ourselves and others.

Remember, prayer is a privilege and a powerful tool in our spiritual journey. Let us embrace it, cultivate it, and allow it to transform us and the world around us.

I leave you with these words from Philippians 4:6-7: "Do not be anxious about anything, but in every situation, by prayer and petition, with thanksgiving, present your requests to God. And the peace of God, which transcends all understanding, will guard your hearts and your minds in Christ Jesus" (ESV).

May you be encouraged to pray without ceasing, knowing that your prayers have a profound impact. May you find peace, strength, and divine guidance through your heartfelt conversations with God.

Be Inspired: Make Bold Moves

DEVOTION 79

Rest

I WANT TO REMIND you of the importance of rest. In our fast-paced world, it's easy to get caught up in the busyness and demands of life. But amidst it all, we must remember to prioritize rest and rejuvenation.

Rest is not a sign of weakness or laziness; it is a necessary part of maintaining our well-being and allowing ourselves to recharge. It is in moments of rest that we find clarity, peace, and the energy to continue on our journey.

When we choose to rest, we give ourselves permission to step away from the constant hustle and bustle. We create space to reflect, to reconnect with ourselves, and to find inspiration. Rest is not a luxury reserved for a select few; it is a vital component of a healthy and balanced life.

In the midst of our daily responsibilities and commitments, it's essential to carve out time for rest. Whether it's a few moments of solitude, a walk through nature, engaging in a hobby, or simply taking a break from our screens, these moments of rest can be transformative.

By intentionally incorporating rest into our lives, we cultivate a sense of renewal and allow ourselves to show up as our best selves. We become more productive, creative, and resilient. Rest is not an indulgence; it is an investment in our well-being and overall effectiveness.

Let us prioritize rest in our lives. Let us embrace moments of stillness and allow ourselves to be refreshed. Find what brings you joy and peace, and make time for it. Let us create a rhythm of rest that supports our physical, emotional, and spiritual well-being.

Remember, rest is not a luxury; it is a necessity. Embrace it, cherish it, and let it restore your soul. As you rest, may you find renewed strength, clarity, and a deep sense of peace.

Take a moment to breathe, to let go of the pressures and worries of the day. Allow yourself to rest, knowing that you are worthy of the gift of rejuvenation. May you be filled with peace and find joy in the stillness.

Rest well, and may you be refreshed for the journey ahead.

Be Inspired: Make Bold Moves

_____
_____
_____
_____
_____
_____
_____
_____
_____
_____
_____
_____
_____
_____
_____
_____
_____
_____
_____
_____
_____
_____
_____
_____
_____
_____
_____

DEVOTION 80

Unwavering Determination

IT'S TIME FOR US to take a stand and pursue our dreams with unwavering determination. Let us not be swayed by the opinions or judgments of others. We must break free from the chains that hold us back and embrace our true potential.

Remember the Scripture from Isaiah 52:1-2, which speaks of removing the chains from our necks. It's a powerful metaphor for breaking free from the limitations and doubts that hinder our progress. We often let fear of judgment or failure paralyze us, but it's time to overcome those obstacles.

Pursue your dreams despite challenges. Ignite the fire within to go after what you truly desire. The time is now. Believe in yourself and your abilities.

When we share our testimonies and past experiences, we open doors for others to find strength and encouragement in their own journeys. Don't be afraid to speak up and share how you overcame obstacles. Your story can inspire others to persevere and believe in themselves.

As we move forward, let's plant seeds of hope, dreams, and purpose. Every action we take today has the potential to grow into something remarkable. Trust that God is guiding us and that our steps are ordered by Him.

Let's applaud the resilience and determination of everyone, and celebrate the dreams and visions that still lie within each of us, regardless of age. Let us press on, knowing that as long as we have breath in our bodies, there is more to accomplish, more to experience, and more to contribute to the world.

Together, let's embrace our dreams, share our stories, and make a difference. The world is waiting for us to rise up and shine.

Be Inspired: Make Bold Moves

DEVOTION 81

Spark Change Together

TAKE THIS DAY TO brainstorm innovative ways to enhance the voting process. Whether it's the idea of having food trucks stationed at polling locations or any other creative suggestions, please think through some ideas and share within your community and consider ways you can collaborate, plan, and strategize, harnessing the collective wisdom and creativity. Collaborate with fellow community members to plan and strategize, harnessing the collective wisdom and creativity of our community.

Let's inspire active involvement in this crucial endeavor. Together, we'll remain in solidarity, taking purposeful steps and effecting meaningful change within our communities. United, we hold the power to instigate positive transformations.

Be Inspired: Make Bold Moves

DEVOTION 82

Embracing Unity, Love, and Truth in a Divisive World

IT'S TIME FOR OUR society to come together, just as thousands gathered in the book of Acts to hear the Word and find salvation. We must unite and stand strong, undeterred by the potential backlash for speaking the truth.

It's disheartening to hear that some believe a person can't be a Christian if they align with a particular political party or agenda. This misconception has persisted for too long. Jesus was inclusive and radical in His love and teachings, calling us to love one another and stand up for justice and truth.

I encourage my fellow believers not to shy away from proclaiming their faith and speaking the truth. Let's rise above divisive rhetoric and embody the love of Christ in our words and actions. Engage in respectful conversations and seek understanding, even with those who have different political views.

I also urge unity among us. If you see me facing attacks on social media, your support and prayers are appreciated. Despite our differences, we are part of the body of Christ. Together, we can overcome division and bring about positive change.

Remember, speaking truth doesn't mean forsaking love and compassion. We can boldly proclaim the truth while extending grace and understanding to others. Let's strive for unity and work towards a society that reflects the values of the Kingdom of God.

I'm committed to this journey and invite you to join me. Together, we can make a difference, one step at a time.

Be Inspired: Make Bold Moves

_____

_____

_____

_____

_____

_____

_____

_____

_____

_____

_____

_____

_____

_____

_____

_____

_____

_____

_____

_____

_____

_____

_____

_____

_____

_____

_____

_____

DEVOTION 83

Prayer and Voting: Harnessing the Power of Faith and Action

I WANT TO EMPHASIZE the power of prayer and the importance of using our voice through voting. The Scripture reminds us that the prayers of the righteous avail much (James 5:16). Prayer has the ability to bring about change, to bring comfort, and to align our hearts with God's will.

In times of uncertainty, and with each election, it is crucial that we turn to prayer. Instead of operating out of fear or frustration, let us be still and pray. Let us seek guidance, discernment, and wisdom from God. Let us pray for righteousness, justice, and unity to prevail.

Prayer alone is not enough; we must also take action. We must not be complacent or allow fear to hold us back. It is our responsibility as citizens to exercise our right to vote. Voting is a powerful way to make our voices heard and to contribute to the shaping of our society.

When we vote, we participate in the democratic process and have a say in the decisions that impact our lives and communities. It is through voting that we can support leaders who align with our values, advocate for policies that promote equality and justice, and bring about positive change.

I understand that some may feel disillusioned or disheartened by the choices presented in an election. However, it is important to remember that not voting only serves to silence our voices and diminish our ability to influence change.

Let us not take our right to vote for granted. Instead, let us educate ourselves on the candidates, their platforms, and the issues at stake. Let us engage in respectful conversations and share our perspectives with others. Let us encourage and empower those around us to exercise their right to vote as well.

Together, through prayer and action, we can make a difference. We can shape the future of our nation and contribute to a more just and compassionate society. Let us pray, let us vote, and let us stand up for what we believe in. Our voices matter, and our actions have the potential to bring about meaningful transformation.

Be Inspired: Make Bold Moves

DEVOTION 84

Faith Over Fear

I WANT TO INSPIRE you to choose faith over fear. Fear has a way of holding us back, paralyzing us from taking action and moving forward. It stifles our potential and limits our ability to pursue our dreams and goals.

But here's the truth: you have the power to choose. You can choose faith over fear. You can choose to believe in yourself, in your abilities, and in the greater possibilities that lie ahead. It's not always easy, and fear may still try to creep in, but it's important to remember that fear is often just a product of our imagination, based on what we perceive as potential risks and uncertainties.

Instead of allowing fear to control your decisions and actions, I encourage you to embrace faith. Have faith in yourself, in your capabilities, and in the resilience within you. Have faith that you are capable of overcoming challenges and achieving your goals. Have faith that there are opportunities waiting for you, even in the face of uncertainty.

Choose faith because faith empowers you. It gives you the courage to step out of your comfort zone, to take risks, and to pursue your passions. It opens doors to new experiences, growth, and personal fulfillment.

When fear tries to hold you back, remind yourself of your inherent strength and resilience. Surround yourself with positive influences and support systems that uplift and encourage you. Practice self-care and self-compassion, nurturing your mind, body, and spirit. Seek inspiration from others who have faced and conquered their fears, knowing that if they can do it, so can you.

Remember, life is too short to let fear dictate your choices and limit your potential. Choose faith, believe in yourself, and step forward with confidence. Embrace the journey ahead, knowing that you have the power to overcome obstacles and achieve your dreams. Have faith, and watch as the possibilities unfold before you.

Be Inspired: Make Bold Moves

_____
_____
_____
_____
_____
_____
_____
_____
_____
_____
_____
_____
_____
_____
_____
_____
_____
_____
_____
_____
_____
_____
_____
_____
_____
_____
_____

DEVOTION 85

Kindness

EMBRACE KINDNESS AND UNITY instead of harboring hate or engaging in divisive behavior. It is disheartening to witness the negativity and criticism directed towards individuals who are making positive contributions to society.

Each of us has been called to fulfill our unique assignments in this world, and it is not for us to judge or hate others who are pursuing their own paths. Instead, let us pause and reflect on why we might feel the need to hate or belittle someone's accomplishments. Are our actions driven by jealousy, insecurity, or a lack of understanding?

Just like Esther in the Bible, who was chosen for a specific purpose in a specific time, each of us has a role to play in the grand scheme of things. Our individual assignments are not for others to dictate or criticize. Rather than wasting energy on negativity, let us focus on fulfilling the assignment that God has given us.

We must understand that we are all interconnected, and our collective purpose is to work together to bring about positive change. It is time to put aside hate and divisive attitudes and come together to fulfill the assignments given to us for such a time as this.

I call upon each of you to take action and join forces in completing the assignments that God has placed before us. Let us cultivate kindness, respect, and unity in our interactions with one another. Instead of tearing each other down, let us build each other up, recognizing that we are stronger together.

Remember, the world needs our collective efforts, diverse talents, and unique perspectives to make a lasting impact. Embrace the truth that we are all chosen for a purpose, and let us fulfill our assignments with humility, compassion, and love. Together, we can create a better world for such a time as this.

Be Inspired: Make Bold Moves

DEVOTION 86

Nurturing Wisdom and Community

IN OUR QUEST TO build a resilient and compassionate community, let us recognize the immense wellspring of wisdom at our disposal. The Scriptures, with their timeless teachings, remind us that if we ever find ourselves in need of guidance, we can ask, and it shall be given to us.

In the present, we stand at a pivotal juncture, grappling with the multifaceted challenges of modern society. Issues like gentrification have left many people displaced from the homes they held dear, driven out by exorbitant property taxes, healthcare costs, and inflation. These individuals often end up in unfamiliar, low-income areas, struggling to connect with their newfound communities. It's precisely here that we can step in as advocates, extending a helping hand, sharing resources, forging connections, and offering much-needed support.

Crucially, we must actively seek the information and guidance necessary to amplify the voices of those we advocate for. Our pursuit of wisdom equips us to make informed decisions that harmonize with our values and envision a brighter future. Remember, wisdom isn't confined to the mere accumulation of facts; it's the art of applying knowledge with discernment, coupled with decisive action.

As you embark on your quest for wisdom, may it empower you and inspire others to follow suit, fortifying our commitment to nurturing a more just and compassionate society. Together, let us be architects of a community built on understanding, compassion, and support.

Be Inspired: Make Bold Moves

DEVOTION 87

Truth

I WANT TO INSPIRE you to be a beacon of truth. In a world filled with misinformation, half-truths, and spin, it is crucial that we stand up for the truth and communicate it with clarity and honesty.

Be the voice that cuts through the noise and delivers the facts. Educate yourself on important issues, dig deeper beyond surface-level information, and seek out multiple reliable sources. When you have a solid understanding of the truth, share it with others in a way that is accessible and understandable.

Avoid the temptation to spin or manipulate the truth to fit a particular narrative or agenda. The truth is powerful on its own, and it has the ability to resonate with people when presented authentically. Speak with integrity and let your words reflect the truth that you hold.

Remember, the truth matters. It has the power to enlighten, unite, and empower. By standing up for the truth, you contribute to creating a more informed and engaged society. You have the opportunity to educate others, inspire critical thinking, and foster meaningful discussions that lead to positive change.

In this time of heightened importance around voting and crucial decisions, let the truth be your guiding light. Be the truth-bearer, the advocate for transparency, and the promoter of honest dialogue. Your commitment to truth will not only impact those around you but will also shape the world we live in.

Embrace the responsibility to be a messenger of truth. Stay informed, speak up, and encourage others to seek and embrace the truth. Together, let us create a culture where the truth is valued, respected, and upheld.

Be Inspired: Make Bold Moves

DEVOTION 88

Joy

FIND JOY IN YOUR life, no matter the circumstances. Joy has the power to transform your perspective and bring a sense of lightness and peace to your everyday experiences. It's easy to get caught up in the challenges and difficulties of life, but when you intentionally seek out joy, it can make a remarkable difference.

Tap into the joy that comes from within, that inner wellspring of joy that can only be found in a deep connection with your faith, your passions, and the things that bring you happiness. For me, as a believer, I find my joy in my relationship with Jesus. I hold onto the truth that the joy of the Lord is my strength. It's a reminder that even in the midst of struggles, I can find strength and resilience through the joy that comes from my faith.

In a world filled with constant news updates, pressures, and challenges, it's crucial to prioritize self-care and intentionally tap into joy. Take breaks, step back, and engage in activities that bring you joy. It could be spending time with loved ones, pursuing hobbies, enjoying nature, or simply doing something that makes your heart sing.

Remember, joy is not dependent on external circumstances. It's an internal state of being that you can cultivate and nurture. Choose to find joy in the small things, appreciate the beauty around you, and approach each day with a grateful heart. When you operate in joy, you radiate positivity, attract positive experiences, and inspire others to do the same.

Make a conscious decision to operate in joy. Embrace the joy that comes from your faith, your passions, and the simple pleasures of life. Let joy be your guiding light, your source of strength, and your perspective-shifter. Find joy, cherish it, and let it shine brightly in everything you do.

Be Inspired: Make Bold Moves

DEVOTION 89

Pause. Reflect. Breathe.

PAUSE, REFLECT, AND BREATHE. In the fast-paced world we live in, it's easy to get caught up in the busyness and forget to take a moment for ourselves. But it's crucial that we intentionally create space to pause, to slow down, and to observe what's happening around us.

When we pause, we give ourselves the opportunity to assess our actions and evaluate if we're truly aligned with our values and purpose. It's a time to reflect on where we've come from, the lessons we've learned, and the growth we've experienced. Reflecting allows us to gain clarity and perspective, and it empowers us to make conscious choices moving forward.

And as we pause and reflect, we must also remember to breathe. Taking deep, intentional breaths helps us to center ourselves, release stress and tension, and reconnect with our inner peace. It's a reminder to prioritize self-care and to nourish our mind, body, and soul.

In the midst of all the noise, distractions, and information overload, pausing, reflecting, and breathing become essential practices for maintaining balance, clarity, and well-being. It's in these moments of stillness that we can realign ourselves with our purpose, find inspiration, and make a positive impact on our communities and the world.

I encourage you to embrace the power of pausing, reflecting, and breathing. Make it a regular practice in your life. Give yourself the gift of slowing down, of gaining perspective, and of nurturing your well-being. In doing so, you'll find renewed clarity, inner peace, and the ability to navigate life's challenges with grace and resilience. Remember, it's okay to take a step back and care for yourself. Pause, reflect, and breathe.

Be Inspired: Make Bold Moves

DEVOTION 90

Power of Praise

PRAISE BREAK! EVEN IN the midst of challenging times, we must choose to bless the Lord and let His praise be continually in our mouths. It is during these dark moments that our praise becomes even more significant.

Praising God doesn't mean denying the difficulties or pretending that everything is perfect. It means acknowledging His greatness, His faithfulness, and His sovereignty in the midst of our struggles. When we lift our voices in praise, we shift our focus from the problems to the One who holds the solution.

Praise has a way of lifting our spirits, renewing our hope, and reminding us of God's unfailing love and provision. It is a powerful weapon against despair, fear, and discouragement. As we praise, we invite God's presence into our lives, and He fills us with His peace and joy.

In every season, in every circumstance, let us make a conscious effort to bless the Lord. Let us cultivate a heart of gratitude and worship. Even when we are weary, let us choose to lift our voices and declare His goodness. As we do so, we will find strength, comfort, and renewed faith in God's unfailing promises.

I encourage you that no matter what you are facing, praise your way through. Lift up your voice, sing, worship, and magnify the Lord. Let His praise be continually in your mouth, and watch as He transforms your perspective, fills you with His peace, and brings breakthrough in your life.

Remember, you are never alone, and God is worthy of all our praise.

Be Inspired: Make Bold Moves

DEVOTION 91

Stand for Something

I URGE YOU TO stand for something. Just as Hannah in the book of 1 Samuel took a stand for herself, it's time for us to rise up and make our voices heard. It can be disheartening when we face obstacles and roadblocks along the way, but we must not lose our resolve.

Taking a stand means standing up for what we believe in, speaking out against injustice, and advocating for positive change. It means refusing to stay silent and passive in the face of adversity. We have a responsibility to make a difference, to be the voice for the voiceless, and to fight for what is right.

Standing for something requires courage, perseverance, and determination. It may not always be easy, and there will be challenges along the way, but the impact we can make is immeasurable. Our actions and words have the power to inspire others and create a ripple effect of change.

Let us take a stand for equality, for justice, for compassion, for love. Let us use our voices to uplift others, to challenge the status quo, and to create a better world. Together, we can make a difference. Stand up, speak out, and let your actions align with your convictions. The time to take a stand is now.

Be Inspired: Make Bold Moves

_____
_____
_____
_____
_____
_____
_____
_____
_____
_____
_____
_____
_____
_____
_____
_____
_____
_____
_____
_____
_____
_____
_____
_____
_____
_____

DEVOTION 92

Press Forward

I ENCOURAGE YOU TO press forward towards the prize for which God has called you. It is time to press on with determination and perseverance, knowing that there is a reward awaiting you. In Christ Jesus, we have the strength and the grace to press through challenges, obstacles, and discouragement.

Pressing towards the prize means staying focused on your purpose and not allowing distractions to deter you. It means pushing past doubts and fears, believing that God has a specific plan and calling for your life. Pressing time is a time to give your best effort, to strive for excellence, and to remain committed to fulfilling God's purpose for you.

Remember that the journey may not always be easy, but the prize is worth it. Stay rooted in your faith, drawing strength from the Lord, and trust that He will guide you and equip you for every step of the way. Press on with confidence, knowing that God has called you and has equipped you to fulfill His purposes.

Let us press forward together, knowing that as we press towards the prize, we are aligning ourselves with God's divine plan. Keep your eyes fixed on the goal, and with perseverance and faith, you will reach the prize that God has prepared for you. Press on, for the time to press is now.

"I'm not saying that I have this all together, that I have it made. But I am well on my way, reaching out for

Christ, who has so wondrously reached out for me. Friends, don't get me wrong: By no means do I count myself an expert in all of this, but I've got my eye on the goal, where God is beckoning us onward—to Jesus. I'm off and running, and I'm not turning back" (Philippians 3:12-14, MSG).

Be Inspired: Make Bold Moves

DEVOTION 93

Hand and Heart

LET OUR HANDS BE vessels of God's purpose, firmly grounded in His divine guidance. As we utter these words, we invite His presence to align our efforts with His greater design. When God establishes the work of our hands, it bestows upon our daily tasks a profound sense of purpose. Our trust in Him deepens, and our actions become a testament to His wisdom.

This divine establishment serves as a compass, helping us strike a balance, uphold noble motives, and refrain from idleness. It teaches us to depend on God's strength, recognizing that our endeavors can impact the lives of others in ways we may not fully grasp.

The ceaseless influx of news and information can be overwhelming, but amid the mayhem, we find solace in turning to God. We implore Him to bless the work we undertake, seeking His guidance in our journey to make a difference.

I laugh at myself every time I mention that news can be overwhelming, but hey, tune in to *News in Motion*. The truth is, even though it can be overwhelming, we can't completely step away from the news. We need it to stay informed about what's happening in the world. Make sure to find a trusted source and consume the news in manageable doses, accompanied by prayer.

Let's extend our hands to those not yet registered to vote, sharing our personal narratives and the profound importance of casting one's ballot. In doing so, we clear away distractions, channeling our collective focus towards the shared purpose of voting—ensuring our voices are not lost in the crowd.

In our pursuit of meaningful change, let us remain steadfast in seeking God's divine establishment for our work. As we align ourselves with His purpose, our actions become a testament to His wisdom and grace. Let diligence, compassion, and intentionality define our commitment to the tasks He has entrusted to us. With every step, may His strength, guidance, and wisdom illuminate our path.

Be Inspired: Make Bold Moves

DEVOTION 94

Seeking Refuge in Christ

THE BOOK *THE 40-DAY Sugar Fast* by Wendy Speake shines truth on our tendency to replace what we've relinquished with other distractions. Whether it's social media, television, constant phone scrolling, or the like, we often opt for new substitutes instead of confronting our addictions head-on.

Rather than addressing the root, we tend to mask it with a fresh alternative. I propose a different approach. When you notice yourself adopting a new habit, whether positive or negative, take a moment to introspect. Ask yourself: "What am I evading? Why not turn to Jesus? What is the source of my hesitation or fear?"

Embracing these questions opens the door to deeper understanding and guides us towards seeking solace, guidance, and strength in the arms of Christ.

By the way, grab a copy of her book—you'll thank me later!

Be Inspired: Make Bold Moves

DEVOTION 95

Embrace Your True Value

GOD HAS BEEN GUIDING me through a profound journey of self-discovery. My recent mantra is, "Grant yourself the freedom to thrive." It's time to cease undermining your own significance. You are not just a survivor; you are an overcomer. Your worth is immeasurable, and you are deserving of acknowledging that.

Luke 12:6-7 reminds us: "Are not five sparrows sold for two pennies? Yet not one of them is forgotten by God. Indeed, the very hairs of your head are all numbered. Don't be afraid; you are worth more than many sparrows."

Let these words sink deep within you. Recognize that God's attention to even the smallest details shows the depth of His care for you. Walk confidently in the truth that you are worth more than you can imagine, and let your actions reflect this inherent value.

Be Inspired: Make Bold Moves

DEVOTION 96

Courageous Persistence

CEASE TRYING TO BESTOW upon others what you think they need; instead, speak courage to their soul.

Deuteronomy 31:6 offers guidance: "Be strong and courageous. Do not be afraid or terrified because of them, for the LORD your God goes with you; he will never leave you nor forsake you." Moses conveyed the same courage to Joshua, affirming that they should venture into the land promised to their ancestors. The Lord would lead and accompany them, banishing fear and discouragement.

These verses remind us that courage is not about avoiding challenges but embracing them, fortified by the knowledge that God walks beside us every step of the way.

Be Inspired: Make Bold Moves

DEVOTION 97

Empowered Liberation

RECLAIMING YOUR POWER IS the key to shifting dynamics. When you regain control, the influence others held over you wanes. This can lead them to lose not only authority over your choices but also potentially their own self-control.

By reasserting your autonomy, you set a precedent that alters the course of interactions. This transformation doesn't just free you, but it can also prompt others to reassess their actions in the absence of the power they once exerted.

Remember, taking back your power is not about dominating others, but about living authentically and without being confined by external forces.

Let's walk in the freedom that God has given to each of us. Let's go!

Be Inspired: Make Bold Moves

DEVOTION 98

Renewal

IN MOMENTS OF QUIET reflection, it's crucial to shed the weight that holds us back. What's hindering your progress? What chains must be loosened? What once propelled you forward but now obstructs your path?

As the seasons shift, it's the ideal time for a "life look." It is a quarterly ritual for me. I encourage you along your journey to seek His guidance on your direction and what you should relinquish to wholeheartedly embrace the journey.

Ask yourself what's causing you to bend beneath its burden. It's time to distinguish between necessary endurance and needless strife. Letting go isn't a display of frailty; it's a stride toward liberation.

Put down the weight that no longer serves you. Rise tall, unburdened, and let your onward journey be characterized by rejuvenated purpose and unhindered steps.

Be Inspired: Make Bold Moves

DEVOTION 99

Persist without Weariness

IN THIS MOMENT, MY message resonates with the call for unwavering perseverance. Read the following Bible verse that speaks to my heart. Galatians 6:9 is the anchor I offer you, "Let us not become weary in doing good, for at the proper time we will reap a harvest if we do not give up."

We find ourselves in a time where weariness creeps in, where the challenges seem insurmountable, and where the world's events often drain our spirits. However, we must not allow weariness to dictate our actions. The verse reminds us to press on with our efforts, to continue sowing goodness even when it feels daunting.

We've encountered hurdles, from elections to clashing opinions, but our commitment to justice must remain strong. This isn't the time for silence or surrender; it's the time for persistence. Your fight might differ from others', but within your unique abilities lies the power to make a difference.

Yes, we're tired, but let's draw strength from our cause. Remember, self-care is vital as well. As we navigate through the noise, let's preserve our energy to tackle the battles that truly align with our purpose. And as we encounter divisive rhetoric and misinformation, let's stay grounded in truth and wisdom.

Let's be vigilant in our fight. Let's not grow faint, for there's much good yet to be sown. As we face this journey, may our endurance be a testament to our commitment.

Be Inspired: Make Bold Moves

DEVOTION 100

Answering God's Call to Love

IN JOHN 14:23-24, JESUS makes a profound statement, expressing that if we love Him, we will obey His teachings found throughout the Bible. He states, "Anyone who loves me will obey my teaching." Therefore, just as He questioned Peter in John 21:15, I believe He is asking each of us today, "Do you love Me?"

"Do you love me?" His message is clear—love and obedience are intertwined. When we truly love God, we naturally obey His teachings, and in return, we find His love and presence in our lives.

Loving those who oppose us or hold different beliefs can be challenging. However, these verses emphasize that love is the cornerstone of our faith. By following Jesus' teachings, we demonstrate our love for Him and open our hearts to God's love.

When you encounter those who may stand against you, remember this divine question. Let your love be a reflection of God's love, boundless and forgiving, even in the face of opposition. In doing so, we not only answer God's question but also embrace the essence of our faith.

Be Inspired: Make Bold Moves

DEVOTION 101

Vetting News Sources

IN AN AGE MARKED by a deluge of misinformation and disinformation, it's become increasingly common for many individuals to disengage from news consumption due to the pervasive negativity that dominates headlines. However, I advocate for a different approach: consistently engage with a reliable news source. Balancing the preservation of your inner peace with the necessity of staying informed is paramount. To do so, you must learn how to assess the trustworthiness of your chosen news source and diligently fact-check the information you encounter.

To evaluate a news source, initiate your assessment with a fundamental online search to acquire information about the source you're scrutinizing. This initial step is vital in determining the source's credibility. Delve further to investigate whether the source upholds ethical standards, as reputable news organizations emphasize fairness, accuracy, and editorial independence. Assess their transparency; credible news sources are known for their openness about their reporting practices, ownership, and financial backing. Check whether the source acknowledges its errors and actively works to rectify them. This willingness to take responsibility for mistakes is a hallmark of credible journalism.

A comprehensive understanding of a source's credibility can be gained by critically examining multiple news articles produced by the source. When evaluating the credibility of a news source, it's important to be alert to any red flags that may indicate the need to seek alternative sources for accurate news. Such red flags include the dissemination of false or untrue content, the use of clickbait tactics, a lack of balance in reporting, the presence of manipulated images or videos, the promotion of state-run or state-sponsored propaganda, and the publication of dangerous, offensive, and malicious content.

It is imperative to bear in mind that while credible sources are not infallible, they are significantly more likely to provide accurate information. In the age of abundant online information, being able to recognize these general indicators of credibility and exercising caution when encountering sources with red flags will substantially enhance your ability to access trustworthy news.

Be Inspired: Make Bold Moves

DEVOTION 102

You Are Free

CHRIST HAS LIBERATED US for a purpose—to work freely, to serve our community with hearts unburdened. So stand steadfast, ensuring you're not bound once more by the chains of servitude.

In Galatians 5:1, we are reminded that Christ has set us free, and this freedom has a purpose. We should stand firmly in this freedom, using it to work, serve, and contribute to our community without being weighed down again by the enslavement of our past.

Be Inspired: Make Bold Moves

DEVOTION 103

Strength in Community: A Call for Collaboration

GRASSROOTS ORGANIZING, A NOBLE and often demanding endeavor, holds the potential to enact profound change within communities. Yet, in the pursuit of this worthy mission, many well-intentioned individuals find themselves standing alone, vulnerable to the burnout that can accompany such a solitary path.

The truth is, we were never meant to journey alone. It's a fundamental principle that runs through the tapestry of human existence. As you engage in the tireless work of grassroots organizing, remember that it takes a community to bring about lasting change.

The All-Important Call to Collaboration. At times, it's easy to believe that shouldering the burden alone is a mark of true dedication. However, God's design for humanity emphasizes collaboration, not isolation. In your commitment to this cause, it's vital to remember that it's not only okay to seek help and collaboration but absolutely necessary.

Turning to God for Guidance. When you feel overwhelmed by the weight of your mission, take time to turn to God. Seek His guidance, strength, and discernment. As you wait for His instructions, you open the door to divine wisdom and insight. God's hand is readily extended to guide you through the complexities of your work.

Collaboration: The Key to Endurance. You may wonder how to identify the right individuals to collaborate with. Trust in God's timing and wisdom. He knows precisely who should walk this journey with you. By seeking His guidance, you can identify those whose skills, passion, and vision align with your own.

In the realm of grassroots organizing, collaboration is more than a strategy; it's a lifeline. Through partnership, you can pool resources, share burdens, and inspire one another. Together, you'll find the strength to endure through the most challenging of times.

Remember, you're part of a greater community, both earthly and divine, that is committed to ushering in positive change. Embrace collaboration, and know that by working hand in hand with those who share your passion, you'll have the strength to weather the storms and savor the victories.

As you navigate the intricate web of grassroots organizing, may God's guidance light your path and lead you to the remarkable individuals with whom you'll collaborate. Through this collective effort, your impact will be amplified, and the prospect of burnout will fade as you lean into the strength of community.

Be Inspired: Make Bold Moves

DEVOTION 104

Setting Your Heart Right

IN 1 JOHN 2:15-17, we are reminded not to become enamored with the world and its fleeting attractions. Loving the world can distract us from the love of our Father. The world often entices us with the desires of the flesh, the lust of the eyes, and the pride of life. These desires, though momentarily appealing, do not align with the will of our Father but are products of the worldly nature.

Instead, we are encouraged to focus on doing the will of God, for this is the path to eternal fulfillment. The world and its desires are temporary, destined to pass away, but those who align themselves with God's will find lasting purpose and eternal life. Let this be a call to keep your heart centered on God's will and not be entangled in the temporary allure of the world.

Be Inspired: Make Bold Moves

DEVOTION 105

Speak Boldly

IN ISAIAH 58:1-3 WE are urged to raise our voices without restraint, like a triumphant trumpet sounding through the land. The message is clear: we must declare to God's people the errors in their lives, confront the sins within our family of Jacob.

You see, many appear devout, steadfastly studying the Lord's ways, striving for a life of righteousness. They seek divine guidance, desiring the Lord's favor. However, they also voice complaints. They wonder why their fasts go unanswered and their acts of humility seem unnoticed.

This Scripture teaches us that it's not enough to just engage in religious practices. Instead, we should focus on both the bold proclamation of truth and the righteous actions that match our faith. Don't merely speak about righteousness; live it. This devotion encourages you to not only ask the Lord for guidance but to also act in ways that align with His teachings, reminding us that faith requires both a vocal declaration and the embodiment of God's love in our actions.

Be Inspired: Make Bold Moves

DEVOTION 106

Discerning the Spirits

IN THE PURSUIT OF wisdom and understanding, we are guided by several foundational verses.

Proverbs 1:7 reminds us that a deep reverence for the Lord forms the bedrock of genuine knowledge. Those who dismiss wisdom and discipline demonstrate foolishness.

James 1:5 encourages us to seek wisdom from God without reservation. God is the generous giver of wisdom, offering it abundantly to all who ask.

1 John 4:1 warns us not to easily believe every spirit. Instead, we should evaluate the spirits we encounter to determine if they align with God's truth. This caution is vital, as the world is rife with false prophets and misleading influences.

These verses collectively advise us to approach knowledge and understanding with a reverence for God, to ask God for wisdom, and to scrutinize the spirits we encounter. In exercising the spirit of discernment, we nurture a deeper connection with God's wisdom and guidance in our lives.

Be Inspired: Make Bold Moves

DEVOTION 107

What Holds You Back?

"Nevertheless even among the rulers many believed in Him, but because of the Pharisees they did not confess *Him,* lest they should be put out of the synagogue; for they loved the praise of men more than the praise of God" (John 12:42-43, NKJV).

REFLECTING ON JOHN 12:42-43, we confront a fundamental question: What restricts our actions?

In this passage, some leaders believed in Jesus but concealed their faith due to fear of the Pharisees and potential expulsion from the synagogue. The fear of losing human praise outweighed their desire for praise from God.

This narrative encourages us to ponder what holds us back from openly expressing our beliefs and faith. Are we too fearful of societal judgments or potential repercussions to stand firmly in our convictions? It beckons us to evaluate our priorities, emphasizing the significance of God's approval over human validation. Let us examine our fears and choose a path guided by faith rather than anxiety about what the world may say or do.

How frequently do we refrain from engaging in our strengths due to fear, or perhaps we avoid taking a stand because we anticipate backlash from others? It's vital to make the choice to approach Jesus with our concerns and leave with the assurance that God will shield us as long as we remain aligned with His purpose and adhere to His guidance. Let's commit to making bold moves and moving forward rather than remaining stagnant out of fear.

Be Inspired: Make Bold Moves

DEVOTION 108

Tender Guidance

LET'S REFLECT ON ISAIAH 40:11: "He cares for his flock like a shepherd: He gathers the lambs in his arms and carries them close to his heart; he gently leads those that have young." The phrase that particularly resonates is "gently leads."

Contemplating this verse, we're reminded of the compassionate care provided by our heavenly Father. Much like a devoted shepherd looks after his flock, our Lord gathers us near to His heart, safeguarding and gently guiding us. The image of being carried close to His heart beautifully symbolizes His profound love for us. This passage encourages us to place our trust in His guidance, recognizing that He leads us with tenderness. His gentle leadership serves as a comforting presence and guidance in our lives. Let's embrace this truth and find solace in the embrace of our gentle Shepherd.

Be Inspired: Make Bold Moves

DEVOTION 109

Build Up with Words

IN EPHESIANS 4:29, WE'RE reminded of the power our words hold:

> "Don't use foul or abusive language. Let everything you say be good and helpful, so that your words will be an encouragement to those who hear them" (NLT).

This verse teaches us the significance of our words. They possess the incredible power to uplift, encourage, and motivate, just as they can hurt, tear down, or leave lasting scars. Our words are tools that can shape the world around us, either for the better or worse.

As we navigate life, let's be mindful of the words we choose to speak. Instead of using foul or hurtful language, let's opt for speech that is good and helpful, creating an environment where our words become a source of encouragement to all who hear them. Our words have the potential to be a force for good, so let's use them wisely and intentionally.

Be Inspired: Make Bold Moves

DEVOTION 110

Embrace Humility in Community Service

"with all humility and gentleness, with patience, bearing with one another in love" (Ephesians 4:2, ESV).

EPHESIANS 4:2 IMPARTS THE wisdom of humility in community work. It encourages us to embody complete humility and gentleness, to be patient and lovingly bear with one another.

In the realm of service, humility is a guiding light. It reminds us that our actions are not about self-glorification but about the betterment of the community. It encourages us to listen and learn, to be gentle in our approach, and to patiently persevere in the face of challenges.

By embracing humility, we foster an environment where the needs of the community come first, and our efforts are genuinely driven by love and care for one another. In this way, we can truly make a positive impact on the lives of those we serve.

Be Inspired: Make Bold Moves

DEVOTION 111

The Harvest of the Spirit

GALATIANS 5:22 REMINDS US of the fruits of the Spirit. These are the qualities that blossom within us when we nurture our spiritual connection. They're like a rich harvest that blesses our lives and the lives of those we encounter.

Love, the core of these fruits, is a selfless and boundless affection for others. It's followed by **joy**, a happiness rooted not in circumstance but in faith. **Peace** follows, a tranquil heart regardless of life's storms. **Patience** is our perseverance through challenges. **Kindness** shows our compassion and empathy. **Goodness** reflects our moral integrity and upright character. And **faithfulness** is the unwavering loyalty and trustworthiness we uphold.

As we tend to our spiritual garden, nurturing these fruits, they become evident in our actions, thoughts, and interactions. They are the sweet yield of a life cultivated with love and care, reflecting the divine nature within us.

Be Inspired: Make Bold Moves

DEVOTION 112

Embracing Authenticity

"Let love be genuine. Abhor what is evil; hold fast to what is good. Love one another with brotherly affection. Outdo one another in showing honor" (Romans 12:9-10, ESV).

THIS POWERFUL VERSE FROM Romans underscores the significance of authenticity in our interactions and relationships. Sincerity in our love and affection for one another is a fundamental principle.

To be sincere in love means more than just expressing affection; it means acting on it. We are encouraged to recognize the difference between right and wrong, holding firmly to what is good and steering clear of evil.

Furthermore, our love should go beyond mere words; it should be evident in our actions. We should treat each other like family, displaying genuine warmth, kindness, and respect. Moreover, the verse encourages us to strive for outdoing one another in showing honor, an inspiring reminder of the beautiful impact that authenticity and sincere love can have on our lives and those around us.

Be Inspired: Make Bold Moves

DEVOTION 113

Finish Strong

EVERY DAY LET US do our part to finish strong.

Let's dive into the empowering story from 2 Kings 4:1-7. It presents a blueprint for a victorious plan, composed of four pivotal steps:

1. **Assess Your Resources.** Begin by asking yourself, "What do I have?" Recognizing your assets, however limited they may seem, is the first stride towards building an effective plan for advocacy. Often you'll find that you possess more than you initially thought.

2. **Eliminate Distractions.** Just as Elisha told the woman in the story to "close the door," we must block out distractions that can divert our energy from the task at hand. In the realm of advocacy, it's vital to focus on the issues that truly matter.

3. **Take Purposeful Action.** "Do the work" emphasizes the importance of action. Advocacy requires effort and commitment. Once you've identified your resources and removed distractions, act purposefully to achieve your goals.

4. **Persist Until Victory.** The final step is to "finish strong." Advocacy often involves challenging situations and might take time. It's crucial to persist despite the obstacles, for success comes to those who persevere.

This biblical passage serves as a reminder that the path to empowerment and successful advocacy remains rooted in these enduring principles. Reflect upon these steps and let them guide your journey to make a positive impact in the lives of others.

Be Inspired: Make Bold Moves

DEVOTION 114

Time to Soar

THE VERSE FROM ISAIAH 40:31 carries a profound message of renewal and strength: "But those who hope in the LORD will renew their strength. They will soar on wings like eagles; they will run and not grow weary, they will walk and not be faint."

In the journey of advocating on behalf of others, it's easy to become fatigued and disheartened. Yet this Scripture reminds us that our hope in the Divine Source can invigorate us. It's a call to pause and reconnect with the unwavering hope in the Divine. When we do, our strength is replenished, allowing us to rise above life's challenges with the grace and power of eagles.

Just as eagles soar through the skies effortlessly, we too can find a renewed vigor in our advocacy efforts. We'll run with perseverance, undeterred by exhaustion, and walk with a sense of unwavering purpose. This verse is a reminder that in times of weariness, we have a source of strength to draw upon, and it empowers us to continue advocating for others with determination and compassion. Let this message renew your spirit, for in hope and Divine strength, you'll find the endurance to continue the important work of advocacy.

Be Inspired: Make Bold Moves

DEVOTION 115

Human Connection

THE WORDS FROM ROMANS 13:8 are a compelling reminder of the core principle that should guide our lives: "Owe no one anything, except to love each other, for the one who loves another has fulfilled the law" (ESV).

This verse encapsulates the essence of community and human connection. It tells us that our primary debt to one another should be the debt of love. In a world that often measures success by material wealth and financial obligations, this verse encourages us to shift our focus. It challenges us to recognize that the most significant debt we can carry is the debt of compassion, empathy, and love for our fellow human beings.

When we embrace this message, we discover that the foundation of any strong community is the love and support its members offer to one another. It reminds us that love transcends boundaries and unites us in the most profound ways. By loving each other, we are not only fulfilling the law but also creating a world filled with compassion and harmony. Let us strive to owe no one anything except love, for in love, we find the true fulfillment of our purpose in this world.

Be Inspired: Make Bold Moves

DEVOTION 116

Embracing Vulnerability

AS STRANGE AS IT might sound, there are moments when you don't have to be the pillar of strength. Let me clarify this notion.

We often find ourselves shouldering the burden of being "the strong one," the person who remains resolute, unwavering, and dependable for others. But in that determination, we sometimes forget that it's perfectly fine to be weak.

Being weak doesn't equate to giving up or surrendering; it's about acknowledging your vulnerabilities. We all have our breaking points, and it's essential to recognize them. When you embrace your moments of weakness, you permit yourself to lean on others for support, to share your concerns, and to let out the feelings that weigh you down.

In essence, "be weak" means to allow yourself the vulnerability that comes with being human. It's a reminder that you don't always have to bear the world's weight on your shoulders. It's okay to seek help, to admit when you're not okay, and to allow yourself to lean on the strength of others. In this vulnerability, you discover resilience and the beautiful interconnectedness of humanity.

Be Inspired: Make Bold Moves

DEVOTION 117

Embracing Diversity in a Fragmented World

IN A WORLD THAT often feels fractured, where divisions can seem insurmountable, the message of "Be still and know" resonates as a powerful call for unity in diversity. It urges us to pause, reflect, and seek understanding.

Each of us is a unique piece in the mosaic of humanity. Our differences—be it race, culture, beliefs, or experiences—can sometimes appear as fault lines in our global society. But "Be still and know" invites us to recognize that within this diversity lies incredible strength.

When we pause and acknowledge the value of every individual, irrespective of our differences, we create space for empathy and understanding to flourish. It's a reminder that amidst the chaos and division, there is a deeper connection we can all tap into—a shared human experience.

Let's strive to be still, to embrace the diversity that makes our world vibrant and beautiful. As we seek to know one another, we can build bridges, foster understanding, and mend the fractures in our world. This verse beckons us to find unity in diversity, for it's in this harmonious tapestry of differences that we discover the full beauty of the human experience.

Be Inspired: Make Bold Moves

DEVOTION 118

Persevering Love

"Above all, love each other deeply, because love covers over a multitude of sins" (1 Peter 4:8).

FIRST PETER 4:8 DELIVERS a powerful message on the endurance of love. When life presents us with challenges and tests, it's often difficult to maintain our loving nature. However, this verse reminds us that above all else, we should continue to love one another earnestly.

Loving earnestly doesn't mean we ignore flaws or overlook mistakes. Instead, it means we remain steadfast in our care and affection for one another, even when things get difficult. Love is the adhesive that can mend the cracks in relationships and forgive the multitude of sins that can accumulate over time.

By persevering in love, we acknowledge that people are inherently imperfect, ourselves included. It's a commitment to understanding, compassion, and empathy when it's easy to turn away. This verse teaches us that love is a potent force, capable of healing wounds and building bridges, especially during the most trying moments in life.

When you face situations where love is tested, remember that love's resilience is powerful. Embrace the call to love earnestly, and let love cover the multitude of sins, for in love's endurance, we find strength and unity.

Be Inspired: Make Bold Moves

DEVOTION 119

Open Hearts

"Here I am! I stand at the door and knock. If anyone hears my voice and opens the door, I will come in and eat with that person, and they with me" (Revelation 3:20).

THE SCRIPTURE IN REVELATION 3:20 is a beautiful reminder of the importance of opening the door to embrace one another, regardless of our faults. It's a message of hospitality and understanding.

In life, we often come across people who may not be perfect, but then again, who among us is? We all have our faults and imperfections, and sometimes we tend to focus on these blemishes instead of the goodness within each person. However, God encourages us to open our hearts and welcome one another.

Just as Jesus stands at the door and knocks, seeking entry into our lives, we should also extend a hand of acceptance to those around us. This act of kindness can transform lives.

It's easy to shun someone because of their faults, to close the door on them. Yet, what if we took a different approach? What if we welcomed them with open arms, just as Jesus beckons us to open the door for Him?

Embracing others doesn't mean you ignore their imperfections. Instead, it means you acknowledge them but choose to love and accept them regardless. We are all a work in progress, and it's the love and grace of community that helps us grow.

Let's take a moment to reflect on our interactions with others. Are there doors we've closed because of someone's faults? If so, perhaps it's time to open them, to offer love and understanding, and to share a meal, either literally or metaphorically.

As we open our doors to one another, with all our faults and imperfections, we participate in the beautiful act of God's love and acceptance. By doing so, we strengthen our communities, foster growth, and, most importantly, reflect the love that Jesus has for us.

Be Inspired: Make Bold Moves

DEVOTION 120

Wait Patiently

"BUT IF WE HOPE for what we do not yet have, we wait for it patiently" (Romans 8:25). Wait patiently. Yes, that's all I have for today. Sometimes we just need to wait and do so patiently.

Be Inspired: Make Bold Moves

DEVOTION 121

Embrace Your Moments of Weakness

MANY OF US ARE feeling the weight of the world right now. We're tired, exhausted, and we're trying so hard to be strong for everyone, at work, at home, and in our communities. You may have seen my passion for those facing food insecurity, single moms or dads, the foster care system, homelessness, helping those who face domestic abuse or human trafficking, and here's a message that I really want to share with you all: It's okay to be weak sometimes.

We all have moments when we want to cry, when we want to scream, when we want to just let it all out. And that's absolutely fine. It's okay not to be strong all the time. It's okay to be vulnerable, to be human.

In 2 Corinthians 12:9-11, we read, "But he said to me, 'My grace is sufficient for you, for my power is made perfect in weakness.' Therefore, I will boast all the more gladly about my weaknesses, so that Christ's power may rest on me. That is why, for Christ's sake, I delight in weaknesses, in insults, in hardships, in persecutions, in difficulties. For when I am weak, then I am strong."

This verse reminds us that we can find strength in our moments of weakness. It's okay to feel tired, to be exhausted, to be frustrated. We must remember that in our times of struggle, we become a vessel for grace and strength.

I recall my experience when someone very close to me had COVID-19 in 2020. I was trying to be strong for this person, helping them through it, but it was a taxing experience. It was when I allowed myself to be weak, to cry, to show my concern and fear, that I found a deeper connection and a source of renewed strength.

When we try to put on a façade of strength all the time, we're not being true to ourselves, and it can have physical and emotional consequences. Tension in your neck and shoulders, among other places, can manifest. It's crucial to release your stress and to be authentic.

In these trying times, when we see so much pain and suffering around us, it's okay to break down and feel the emotions. When someone asks you how you're doing, it's alright to say, "I'm not okay today." You don't have to put on a brave face all the time. In fact, it's important not to.

And when someone shares their vulnerability with you, respond with empathy and respect. Create a safe space for them to express their feelings. It's a sign of true friendship and compassion.

Life has been exceptionally challenging for several years, and collectively we've been through a lot. Let's not pretend that we're always okay when we're not. Be weak, be genuine, but don't stay there. Find ways to reach out, seek support, and connect with others. We're here as a community to listen and understand. It's okay to be weak, but we'll be strong together.

Be Inspired: Make Bold Moves

_____

_____

_____

_____

_____

_____

_____

_____

_____

_____

_____

_____

_____

_____

_____

_____

_____

_____

_____

_____

_____

_____

_____

_____

_____

_____

_____

DEVOTION 122

Embrace the Power of Increase

HERE'S A MESSAGE ABOUT "increase." I'm not just referring to financial gain; I'm talking about an increase in wisdom, knowledge, and understanding. We find ourselves in a world brimming with information and challenges, and it's vital that we equip ourselves with the insights needed to make a difference.

The first step is to recognize that the power of "increase" goes beyond our personal growth. It's about extending our newfound wisdom and knowledge to our communities. Just as a single candle can ignite many others, your knowledge can illuminate the lives of those around you. It's essential to share what we learn, to help others understand important legislation, or provide resources that can make their lives better.

Find one family to support, even through prayer, silently standing with them, and offering your words of encouragement.

As you embrace the theme of "increase," think not only of your growth but also of the growth you can ignite in your community. Let's sow the seeds of wisdom and knowledge without hesitation. In the end, it's these small contributions that make the most significant difference in the world.

Be Inspired: Make Bold Moves

DEVOTION 123

Embrace Your Victory

HERE IS A REMINDER that God has never lost a battle. This unwavering truth is something we can hold onto, especially during times of uncertainty, like the year 2020 and the challenges life presents us.

It's vital to remember that this victory goes beyond any battle we face; it's a testament to God's power. In the face of adversity, we can find solace in the belief that God never loses a battle, and He never will. As a beautiful song so aptly put it, "He can do all things but fail."

Think back to 2020, consider your own life, your joys, your struggles, your relationships. In all of these, even when things seem bleak, take a moment to remember that God has never lost a battle. Let this thought lead you into a place of worship and thanksgiving, just as it did for me. Shift your perspective to see that no matter how things appear, God will come through, and victory will be yours.

Let's turn to the Word for guidance. It reminds us not to be afraid or discouraged, for the battles we face are not ours alone, but God's. Regardless of the enormity of the challenges, we must hold our heads high, knowing that God has equipped us for this journey.

Whatever your current situation, whether you're questioning your bank account, your food supply, or your job status, trust that God has never lost a battle. Sometimes, challenges are opportunities in disguise, teaching us to rely on Him. He will not fail you. Your victory is assured.

I share a personal story to emphasize the power of God's guidance. In obedience to His calling, my husband and I closed the church God had called us to pastor. This act led to remarkable revelations in our journey. While we were in our own battle, longing to do ministry differently, God had never lost control of our path. We thought it was a lifelong calling, but God never told us we were called to that particular assignment indefinitely. It was a beginning of a larger plan. We learned to surrender, submit, and obey. And guess what? The story didn't end there.

When you feel the vast army of life's challenges closing in, remember that the battle is not yours alone. God is with you. Just wait, and it will work out. You might not see it now, but you will be victorious. Victory awaits, and it's yours to embrace.

God has a unique plan for each of us, and the battles you face are part of that plan. You may not understand it now, but stay faithful, for He can do all things. He has equipped you for victory. Be bold and take that step of faith. Your victory is certain, even when it doesn't seem to make sense.

Let us be inspired by the fact that God has never lost a battle, and He will never lose yours. Victories are born out of faith, and as you step out in faith, you move closer to the triumph that awaits. Remember, the battle is the Lord's, and He never loses. Your victory is assured.

Be Inspired: Make Bold Moves

DEVOTION 124

Embrace Authentic Friendship

A TRUE FRIEND, AN authentic friend, doesn't need to ask for anything in return when they have come alongside of you for whatever the reason, financial or lending an ear or shoulder. They simply give selflessly, without hesitation, and without conditions.

In Proverbs 18:24, we read: "Friends come and friends go, but a true friend sticks by you like family" (MSG). This means that a true friend will stand by your side through thick and thin, no matter the circumstances.

Your true friends can become your lifeline. They're there to support, to lift you up, to lend a shoulder, and to provide a listening ear. They understand that sometimes silence says more than words ever could.

In a world filled with chaos and confusion, we need authentic friendships. These are the kind of friends that don't question or press for answers; they simply stand by your side. They understand that sometimes you're not ready to talk or share your struggles.

An authentic friend knows that you may say "I'm fine" when you're not, and they respect that. They'll reach out, asking, "How are you doing?" Even if you don't want to talk, they'll make sure you know they're there, available whenever you're ready to open up.

True friends offer a helping hand, support you during your struggles, and don't let you bear the burden alone. They're present when it matters most, even when we had to keep our distance due to the pandemic.

In the spirit of "love your neighbor as yourself," let's remember that your neighbors are your friends. Regardless of their current feelings towards you, it's time to express your love and care. These true friendships will be your refuge in troubled times.

It's time to let go of the masks we wear and the weight we carry, releasing ourselves from past hurts and pain. Mental health is vital, and we must find the strength to seek help and share our experiences.

Shed those masks and let your true self shine. Drop the pretense, be free, and open up about your struggles. Our ancestors carried heavy burdens in silence, but now is the time to release the weight.

Family can be your closest friends, and friends can become family. Take the time to reconnect with those you may have distanced yourself from and release any judgments. Let go, forgive, and express your love.

There's a powerful message in helping others who may be battling addictions or hardships. Approach them with love and understanding. We're facing an eviction crisis, and your support could make a world of difference.

Be an authentic friend. Embrace the freedom of forgiveness and reconciliation. Life is too short to hold grudges. Let's be friends, true friends, embracing authenticity and sharing our love.

Be Inspired: Make Bold Moves

DEVOTION 125

Hello

WHAT'S YOUR GREETING? EVERY day we cross paths with countless souls, some familiar and many strangers. What's your greeting? As I delved into Luke chapter 1 today, I was struck by a profound truth: "As soon as the sound of your greeting reached my ears, the baby in my womb leaped for joy." Think about that for a moment. Your greeting can do something incredible; it can make someone's spirit leap.

In a world filled with uncertainty, hidden struggles, and battles we may know nothing about, our greeting has the power to change someone's day. When you put down your phone and take a moment to look someone in the eye to say, "Good morning," "You're beautiful," or "I'm thinking of you," you're not just offering words; you're offering a lifeline.

It's not about the phone, the distraction, or the rush. It's about connecting with others on a profound human level. It's about kindness, empathy, and understanding. As you go about your day, remember the incredible impact your greeting can have. Imagine a world where we're all on our porches, our balconies, waving and sharing greetings of goodwill. It starts with us, with our daily greetings, with the love and respect we offer one another.

What's your greeting today? Reach out, connect, and let your spirit shine. Let your greeting make someone's spirit leap, for in that simple act, you can change the world.

Be Inspired: Make Bold Moves

DEVOTION 126

Self-Denial

LET'S FIND INSPIRATION IN the powerful act of self-denial, a call to #StandTogether in unity. It shows us the power of sacrifice for a greater cause. Let's extend this idea to our communities.

Consider the Thanksgiving season. I know, depending upon when you are reading this book the season may have passed, or you could be approaching that time. Regardless, travel with me for a moment and reflect on the Thanksgiving season. In your reflections, think about those who are hungry, cold, and facing hardships.

Here's the call to action: Think on three things you are thankful for. Now go into your community and help others become just as thankful. Count your blessings, while considering how you can give back. Reflect on what's going well, what needs to change, and how you can serve your community. Together, we can make a difference.

Let's stand with each other, #StandWithCommunity, and create a better future together.

Be Inspired: Make Bold Moves

_____
_____
_____
_____
_____
_____
_____
_____
_____
_____
_____
_____
_____
_____
_____
_____
_____
_____
_____
_____
_____
_____
_____
_____
_____
_____

DEVOTION 127

Encouraging Maturity and Forgiveness

I'D LIKE TO TALK about two essential aspects of our lives—maturity and forgiveness. First, forgiveness. Reflect on the individuals in your life whom you've chosen not to forgive. That unforgiveness might be affecting your well-being. Take a moment to perform some introspection. Ask yourself, "Whom do I need to forgive?" But don't forget to include yourself in this process. It's crucial to release any guilt or shame you might be carrying. It's time to tell yourself, "I forgive you. I release you from this burden."

Now let's address maturity. Maturity involves recognizing your worth and value. When you understand your value and confidence, the negativity others try to impose on you doesn't affect you. When you are more than a conqueror, as the Bible states, and the head and not the tail, it's time to embrace your identity.

It's time to mature and heighten our self-awareness. No, this isn't arrogance; it's knowing your worth as God sees it. If you believe you're more than a conqueror and the head, let others wrestle with why they can't appreciate that. Use it as a mirror for self-reflection.

Maturing and forgiving go hand in hand. As we forgive ourselves and others, we empower ourselves economically. We've been playing small for too long. Break the cycle and embrace the promises and purpose that God has designed for you. It's time to live into your calling.

Be Inspired: Make Bold Moves

DEVOTION 128

Preparedness and Selflessness

TODAY'S INSPIRATIONAL MESSAGE REVOLVES around preparedness, and it may sound somewhat familiar, especially for those who've grown up in church. I vividly recall the Sunday school lessons about being prepared. One thing drilled into my head was how many books there are in the Bible. Yes, there are 66 books, and I can still sing that song in my head. So I pondered what it means to prepare, given the current circumstances, like the makeshift hospitals popping up. I realized that preparation extends beyond gathering supplies.

There are 66 books in the Bible, and when you break it down, there are 27 new and 39 old books, making up the grand total. This made me reflect on how we prepare for the challenging times we face today. The pandemic's severity is evident, and we must prepare ourselves. But how do we prepare?

God showed me that true preparation means embracing selflessness. It means thinking about our neighbors, just as we love ourselves.

Preparation extends to our community. Do I have enough supplies not only for myself but also for those who might need them? Do I have enough food to share if someone comes knocking? Will I offer assistance without hesitation? The readiness we need isn't just for self-preservation; it's about considering others in our community.

As I gather supplies, I'm also preparing to be of service to others. I'm contemplating the needs of the broader community. Can I help my neighbor with a mask? Am I prepared to offer a can of food to someone in need? We must shift our focus away from ourselves and consider how we can serve our community.

We need to break free from selfishness and instead look out for our neighbors. To prepare is to serve. It's time to think beyond ourselves and consider our community. Let's get ready, not just for our own sake, but for the betterment of all.

Be Inspired: Make Bold Moves

_____

_____

_____

_____

_____

_____

_____

_____

_____

_____

_____

_____

_____

_____

_____

_____

_____

_____

_____

_____

_____

_____

_____

_____

_____

_____

DEVOTION 129

Giving and Community Support

THIS INSPIRATIONAL MESSAGE CENTERS around the act of giving. We're in a season where giving should be a constant, though it's especially vital during these times. In the Bible, Luke 6:38 reminds us, "Give, and it shall be given unto you, good measure pressed down, shaken together and running over" (KJV). It's a powerful message about the power of giving.

However, it's essential to look beyond external appearances. People often wear masks, not just for safety but also to hide their struggles. If your heart feels called to help someone, do so. You don't always need to ask if they need assistance. Use your discernment and let your actions speak. Give, whether it's money or food, and you can even leave groceries on someone's doorstep without needing recognition.

As we navigate these challenging times, remember the importance of selflessness. In this season, it's about giving back to your community. For example, consider supporting local businesses and joint ventures. A small subscription to a local gym or organization can make a significant difference.

Lastly, we should ponder the power of giving and voting. While we don't need to give to influence someone's vote, we've seen how impactful voter registration and engagement can be. We should explore innovative ways to promote voting and giving back to the community.

I don't have all the answers, and that's where our collective community comes into play. We need to think collectively about how we can give back, vetting organizations, and individuals to ensure our efforts go towards real change. We're in this together, and together, we can make a difference.

Be Inspired: Make Bold Moves

DEVOTION 130

Forgiveness and Healing

YES, THIS IS ONE of the repeat devotions that I mentioned you may stumble upon as you work through this book. As I stated, sometimes we have to be repetitive. So let's once again talk about the incredible power of forgiveness. Forgiving is not just about letting go of the past; it's about freeing yourself from the chains of unforgiveness. Unforgiveness can be like a relentless disease that infects your body, mind, and soul, often without you even realizing it.

Consider unforgiveness as a deeply rooted weed in the garden of your heart. It may be hidden, and you may try to treat it on the surface, but beneath the soil lies a stubborn root. These roots can be as tough as a massive boulder, silently sapping your strength and holding you back.

Think of it this way: unforgiveness is a stronghold that keeps you from moving forward. Sometimes it even manifests in physical ailments, obesity, depression, or oppression. You might wonder why these issues persist, but the answer could be buried within unforgiveness.

Just like the weeds in your garden that wrap around hidden rocks, unforgiveness takes hold of your spirit, affecting your health and well-being. But the good news is that just like that gardener who uncovered the hidden boulder, you have the power to unearth the stronghold of unforgiveness in your life.

Let's dig deep within ourselves and search for these hidden boulders of unforgiveness. Instead of addressing things only on the surface, let's work on pulling out the roots. By confronting the source of your pain and anger, you can start fresh with a clean slate, ready to move forward.

Consider this in the context of recent events you may have experienced. When it comes to relationships strained by political divisions, can we let go of unforgiveness? Are we willing to have conversations, bridge gaps, and heal wounds rather than holding grudges indefinitely?

The message today is to evaluate your heart and the unforgiveness you may be harboring. It's time to seek understanding, reconciliation, and healing. In this uncertain world, where life can change in an instant, let's start mending broken relationships, addressing our prejudices, and rekindling empathy. Embrace your own healing by releasing the stronghold of unforgiveness. By doing so, you allow yourself to move forward with newfound strength and grace.

Be Inspired: Make Bold Moves

_____
_____
_____
_____
_____
_____
_____
_____
_____
_____
_____
_____
_____
_____
_____
_____
_____
_____
_____
_____
_____
_____
_____
_____
_____
_____
_____
_____

DEVOTION 131

Letting Go and Embracing New Beginnings

I WANT TO TALK to you about the liberating power of letting go. It's time to shed the weight, to release those anchors that are holding you down, and to step into a brighter, more fulfilling future. You see, life is an ever-evolving journey, and sometimes we must reassess our course.

Ask yourself, "What's keeping me from soaring? What's tethering me to a reality I've outgrown? What used to serve me well but now feels like a burden?" It's essential to recognize when a season has passed and your assignment has evolved.

Too often we cling to roles or activities because they define us in some way. They become part of our identity. But here's the revelation: your identity isn't tied to a job title, a financial role, or an obligation. Your identity is inherently good because you're a creation of the Divine. Embrace that truth.

What's fascinating is how we sometimes block our own blessings. We grasp tightly to things, even when their season has passed. We fear releasing them because they may provide some income or recognition. But here's the secret: there might be an open door just waiting for you on the other side.

Don't let fear of the unknown hold you back. Financial concerns, or the desire for titles and material things, shouldn't define your decisions. It's time to listen to that inner voice that calls you toward your passions, your true purpose. Unshackle yourself from what's holding you down.

If God places a new opportunity before you, trust that it's for your greater good. Sometimes we must relinquish the good to embrace the great. Trust that God has more significant plans for you, but you must first make room by letting go of what's no longer serving you.

And remember, you don't owe anyone an explanation for your decisions. You already made a commitment to your higher purpose. Go forward with confidence, knowing that laying aside these weights will empower you, lift your spirit, and create room for the abundant blessings God has in store.

As you shed the old, you'll stand taller, walk more powerfully, and speak with renewed purpose. People will notice the presence of the Divine shining through you, and you'll become a beacon of inspiration for others.

I encourage you to do your own "life look." Examine what's been weighing you down, and be willing to lay it aside. Your future is bright, and there's a world of new beginnings just waiting for you to embrace.

Be Inspired: Make Bold Moves

DEVOTION 132

Let's Talk Healing

IN THESE DIVIDED TIMES, God won't ask who we voted for but rather how we treated our neighbors. Our duty, first and foremost, is to love our neighbors as ourselves. These neighbors can be anyone, regardless of their background or life circumstances.

We must be cautious about making claims that fellow Christians are destined for hell because of their voting choices. Such divisive statements are not in alignment with the truth. We should encourage open dialogue and foster unity, for the greater cause of faith. It's not about who we voted for but how we walked in our faith, how we treated others, and how we lived what we preached.

It's essential to teach the entire Bible, not just selective passages. What we teach from our pulpits, whether in a traditional church or a digital platform, needs to reflect the entirety of God's Word. We should examine the Bible closely through observation, interpretation, and application, seeking wisdom and understanding in how it relates to our lives.

We need to remember that when we stand before God, He won't be concerned with our voting choices but with how well we've walked in love, compassion, and kindness towards our fellow human beings. Let's be cautious about condemning others to hell and instead focus on living out our faith in love, unity, and understanding.

Be Inspired: Make Bold Moves

DEVOTION 133

We Can Adapt

I CAN, YOU CAN, we can. Adjust the plan. Never give up on what you want to do. Sometimes you may need to alter your course a bit, but you should still do it.

Life may not go as planned. The job you didn't get, the relationship that ended, the degree you thought you wanted, or the unexpected obstacles you face; none of these define you. Adjust your plan. Embrace change. My own journey has taken an unexpected path, but I'm having the time of my life.

What about you? How can you adjust your plan to achieve your goals and dreams? #AdjustThePlan

Be Inspired: Make Bold Moves

DEVOTION 134

Reflecting Within

LET'S TAKE A MOMENT to reflect within ourselves. What do you see when you look within? Are you being a team player, or are you isolating on your own island? Are you uplifting others, or are you tearing them down? Are you extending a helping hand, or are you taking from them? What do you see when you look within, and how can you make a difference?

Let's move past judgment and assumptions about others based on their material possessions or circumstances. Look within yourself and ask, "What do I see?" Be the change you want to see in the world.

Be Inspired: Make Bold Moves

_____

_____

_____

_____

_____

_____

_____

_____

_____

_____

_____

_____

_____

_____

_____

_____

_____

_____

_____

_____

_____

_____

_____

_____

_____

_____

DEVOTION 135

Simplicity in Faith: A Life Defined by Micah 6:8

IN THE MIDST OF life's complexities and the multitude of choices we face, God's Word often shines a beacon of simplicity to guide our way. Micah 6:8, as conveyed in *The Message*, offers one such beacon:

> "But he's already made it plain how to live, what to do, what GOD is looking for in men and women. It's quite simple: Do what is fair and just to your neighbor, be compassionate and loyal in your love, and don't take yourself too seriously—take God seriously."

Do What Is Fair and Just. Our journey begins with a call to fairness and justice. These are not just lofty ideals, but practical actions. In our communities, homes, and workplaces, let's strive to treat others with fairness. Seek to right the wrongs you encounter, stand up against injustice, and advocate for the equitable treatment of your neighbors.

Be Compassionate and Loyal in Your Love. Love, in its purest form, is characterized by compassion and loyalty. This love extends beyond romantic feelings to a deep and abiding care for others. Be compassionate towards those who are hurting, and stand by your loved ones through thick and thin. Let your love be an unwavering force that uplifts and supports those around you.

Don't Take Yourself Too Seriously. In the pursuit of justice and compassion, we mustn't forget humility. Life can be complex and challenging, but we should not allow ourselves to be consumed by pride or self-importance. Instead, maintain a spirit of humility and recognize that our ultimate purpose is to serve and honor God.

Take God Seriously. Lastly, as we navigate this simple yet profound path, it's essential to place God at the center of our lives. Take your relationship with Him seriously, prioritize your faith, and allow His wisdom to guide your actions. Seek His guidance in your endeavors, and remember that through Him, the pursuit of fairness, compassion, loyalty, and humility is possible.

In a world often filled with noise and distractions, the simplicity of Micah 6:8 reminds us of our fundamental calling as people of faith. As we strive to do what is fair and just, extend compassion and loyalty, and maintain humility, we embark on a journey that mirrors the heart of God. Take these simple yet powerful principles to heart, for it is in their practice that we find true meaning and purpose in our lives.

Be Inspired: Make Bold Moves

DEVOTION 136

Unstoppable Determination

DON'T LET ANYTHING OR anyone stand in your way.

Don't let anything stand in your way.

Don't let anyone stand in your way.

Now, here's the thing—we all need to be more transparent about what's happening in our lives. If we become more open about our challenges, people will be more willing to share. Disabilities aren't always visible, so don't make assumptions based on appearances. Let's be vulnerable, but not to the point of oversharing.

Be Inspired: Make Bold Moves

_____
_____
_____
_____
_____
_____
_____
_____
_____
_____
_____
_____
_____
_____
_____
_____
_____
_____
_____
_____
_____
_____
_____
_____

DEVOTION 137

Inspiring Resilience: Listen to Your Heartbeat

LET ME MAKE ONE thing perfectly clear—I'm telling you this because I care. It's crucial that you take a moment right now and listen to your heartbeat. Amid all this talk of anxiety and stress, we need to be in tune with our own bodies.

We can't afford to let anxiety overwhelm us during these times. Many are anxious, especially about the new justice. But here's the key: **We can't afford to stress out. We've come too far. We need to breathe, stay resilient, and keep moving.**

Stay strong, stay informed, and keep moving. Let's be bold and unyielding in the face of adversity. Our voices matter, and our actions count.

Be Inspired: Make Bold Moves

DEVOTION 138

Empowering Prayer Warriors

AS I OPEN IN my workbook *Ready to Pray*, I want to pen the same words here.

The stillness of this moment gives us a sense of the presence of the Most High God whispering, "Be still and know that I am God." "Most Holy and Awesome God, how excellent is Your Name in all the earth—the God of love who sits high and looks down below sending blessings and promises to Your children.

I pray in the name of Jesus for the person who is reading this right now. Bless them, Lord. Bless their family, their neighbors, their friends, their coworkers, and even their enemies. God, only You know exactly what each and every person needs. I lift up to You their every concern, their dreams and desires, in this quiet and still moment. God, breathe into Your servant new life. May they find rest in the shadow of the Almighty God! Open up the windows of heaven and pour them out a blessing that they will not have room enough to receive.

I join the apostle Paul in praying Ephesians 3:14-19,

"For this reason I kneel before the Father, from whom his whole family in heaven and on earth derives its name. I pray that out of his glorious riches he may strengthen you with power through his Spirit in your inner being, so that Christ may dwell in your hearts through faith. And I pray that you, being rooted and established in love, may have power, together with all the saints, to grasp how wide and long and high and deep is the love of Christ, and to know this love that surpasses knowledge that you may be filled to the measure of all the fullness of God."

Life today is our reason to pray. Let's stay the course and let's continue to pray.

Be Inspired: Make Bold Moves

_____

_____

_____

_____

_____

_____

_____

_____

_____

_____

_____

_____

_____

_____

_____

_____

_____

_____

_____

_____

_____

_____

_____

_____

_____

_____

_____

_____

DEVOTION 139

Prioritize Self-Care in the Midst of Advocacy

PRIORITIZE SELF-CARE ABOVE ALL else. Protect your personal space, nurture your mental health, and maintain your overall well-being. If the news becomes overwhelming, do not hesitate to switch it off. Be mindful of what you consume, monitor your conversations, and remain vigilant about your emotional state.

To be a pillar of strength in your community, it is essential to prioritize your own well-being. As we strive to connect and support others, building resilience starts with self-care. Begin by praying for one another.

Here are three simple steps for self-care:

1. Practice daily meditation or deep-breathing exercises.
2. Engage in physical activity, such as walking, yoga, or dancing, to promote mental and physical wellness.
3. Set boundaries to protect your time and energy, and learn to say no when necessary.

Be Inspired: Make Bold Moves

_____

_____

_____

_____

_____

_____

_____

_____

_____

_____

_____

_____

_____

_____

_____

_____

_____

_____

_____

_____

_____

_____

_____

_____

_____

_____

_____

DEVOTION 140

Embrace Peace

I DECLARE PEACE, I declare peace. Since the onset of the 2020 pandemic, there's been a noticeable rise in anxiety worldwide. People seem increasingly on edge. Consider for a moment the myriad concerns: children and schooling, parents and work, families, singles, individuals of all ages, the economy, global uncertainty—there's a palpable undercurrent of anxiety. Many ask, "Where did this come from, and why now?"

Countless individuals openly admit to grappling with anxiety for the first time. Did it stem from the isolation during the pandemic? The answer remains elusive, but it's crucial to engage in conversation to foster transparency, support, and ultimately, peace. Once again—I speak peace.

I have a genuine belief that everything will eventually be alright.

My call to you is this—safeguard your space, both mentally and emotionally. I speak peace to your soul. Protect your surroundings, for it's the space where your peace and well-being lie.

And a word to all of you with dreams and aspirations—if you have a calling, a purpose, a dream, please pursue it. The world is vast, and there's a place for you. Even if someone else is already in the field, be at peace and remember, if you know that it's your calling, do it. You are unique, and your voice and purpose matter.

Be Inspired: Make Bold Moves

DEVOTION 141

My Hope in a Divided World

IN PSALM 119:114, WE find assurance in these words: "You are my hiding place and my shield; I hope in Your word" (NKJV). This verse resonates with the idea that our hope is anchored in God's Word, especially in times when the world feels divided and chaotic. When the storms of life, including the storms of division and uncertainty, rage around us, we find solace in His promises, which provide both shelter and protection. Our hope, firmly rooted in these promises, becomes a beacon of light in a world that often feels divided. It's a reminder that amidst the discord, we can find unity in our shared hope in God's unwavering Word.

Be Inspired: Make Bold Moves

_____

_____

_____

_____

_____

_____

_____

_____

_____

_____

_____

_____

_____

_____

_____

_____

_____

_____

_____

_____

_____

_____

_____

_____

_____

_____

_____

DEVOTION 142

Abounding Joy in Advocacy

JAMES 1:2-3 ENCOURAGES US to find joy, even when advocating in our community, and to maintain that joy when faced with struggles: "Consider it pure joy, my brothers and sisters, whenever you face trials of many kinds, because you know that the testing of your faith produces perseverance." It's a reminder that through life's challenges and the challenges of advocating for positive change, our faith is strengthened, and with faith comes the ability to endure and overcome. This endurance, developed through advocacy, becomes a source of profound and abounding joy. It's a reminder that our efforts for a better world can bring immense happiness, even in the face of adversity.

Be Inspired: Make Bold Moves

_____
_____
_____
_____
_____
_____
_____
_____
_____
_____
_____
_____
_____
_____
_____
_____
_____
_____
_____
_____
_____
_____
_____
_____
_____
_____

DEVOTION 143

A Patient Wait in the Face of Gentrification

PSALM 130:5 REMINDS US of the virtue of patience: "I wait for the LORD, my whole being waits, and in his word I put my hope." In the context of gentrification and the pressing need for neighborhoods to take care of marginalized residents, patience becomes a valuable asset. As communities face rapid changes and uncertainties, the act of waiting can transform into a period of hopeful anticipation, trust in one another, and personal growth. It's a reminder that as we address the challenges of our times, such as gentrification, patience and hope in unity can help us take care of all community members, especially those marginalized, and work toward a better, more inclusive future.

Be Inspired: Make Bold Moves

DEVOTION 144

The Power of Unyielding Faith in Times of Adversity

HEBREWS 11:1 BEAUTIFULLY ENCAPSULATES the profound nature of faith: "Now faith is the assurance of things hoped for, the conviction of things not seen" (ESV). This Scripture resonates deeply with the challenges many individuals face today, from lack and food insecurity to homelessness, health issues, job losses, and inflation. In the realm of advocacy, community building, and voter education, faith becomes an anchor for our determination to hold elected officials accountable.

Even when circumstances appear bleak, faith serves as our unwavering conviction that positive change is attainable. It's the invisible thread that links our aspirations to our actions, reassuring us that the better future we hope for is not only possible but inevitable. In our collective efforts to address these complex issues and create a more inclusive society, faith empowers us to persist, knowing that our work is both meaningful and transformative.

Be Inspired: Make Bold Moves

DEVOTION 145

The Transformative Power of Your Words

BISHOP TD JAKES WISELY reminds us in his sermon series, "Crushing," "Change the way you talk to yourself, or you will always be where you have always been. We have to put Word on word." This insight underscores the profound influence of our words and thoughts on our lives. The power of life and death, as the Scriptures affirm, resides in the tongue. Let us choose our words wisely.

As we engage in discussions surrounding advocacy, community development, and the essential need for voter education, our language takes center stage. It is vital to steer our conversations away from negativity and instead let our words become vehicles for change, draped in passion and purpose. We speak not just for ourselves but also for the creation of transformed neighborhoods where everyone has access to essentials like food, clothing, and jobs.

We advocate for elected officials who prioritize the needs of their constituents over profits. Our words carry the potential to shape a brighter, more equitable future. Let us use them to breathe life into our ideals and aspirations. As we watch what we say, we manifest the change we long to see in our communities and society at large.

Proverbs 18:21 reminds us, "Death and life are in the power of the tongue: and they that love it shall eat the fruit thereof" (KJV). Let's pledge to speak life to both ourselves and others. Here's a call to action: embark on a 21-day journey of speaking only positive affirmations to yourself. Even in challenging circumstances, choose to speak life instead of death.

For example, "Though my neighborhood is undergoing gentrification and I may lack the financial means to buy multiple homes in the area, I'm dedicated to taking proactive measures. This includes attending community meetings and engaging with local representatives to advocate for housing solutions for displaced individuals."

It's one thing to sit back and do nothing, wishing you had done something. It's another to accept the call to action and do what you can while reaching out to others within the community. The goal is to speak life rather than death into any situation, regardless of how it may appear.

Be Inspired: Make Bold Moves

DEVOTION 146

Fear Not: A Voice for Change

IN JOSHUA 10:25, WE are reminded, "Do not be afraid; do not be discouraged. Be strong and courageous." These timeless words resonate deeply, especially in the context of advocating for change, human rights, civic engagement, and speaking up for justice.

The path to transformation often demands that we raise our voices, participate in the democratic process, attend town hall meetings, and advocate for human rights and equality. In these endeavors, fear can be a lurking shadow, discouraging us from taking action.

However, Joshua's wisdom reminds us that fear should not deter us. Instead, it should empower us to be strong and courageous in our efforts for change. By confronting our fears, we become resilient advocates, capable of driving transformation and creating a more just and equitable world.

As we stand up for what's right, let us carry Joshua's words in our hearts. Let us not be afraid, nor discouraged, but resolute in our commitment to be strong and courageous voices for change.

Be Inspired: Make Bold Moves

DEVOTION 147

Embrace the Opportunity to Serve

IN OUR DAILY LIVES, we often encounter numerous opportunities to serve our community, although sometimes they might be subtle or easily overlooked. In Matthew 25:40, Jesus said, "Truly, I say to you, as you did it to one of the least of these my brothers, you did it to me" (ESV). This verse highlights the significance of serving others, especially those in need.

Each day we can find these chances to make a difference. It could be as simple as helping a neighbor with their groceries, volunteering at a local shelter, mentoring a young person, or participating in a community cleanup. These acts of kindness are like seeds planted in the soil of your community. They have the potential to grow into beautiful expressions of love and care.

Don't underestimate the power of your actions. Every small act of service contributes to the well-being of your community and can create a ripple effect of positive change. When we embrace these opportunities, we live out Jesus' teaching, understanding that by serving others, we serve Him.

Keep your heart open to the opportunities that come your way. Seize each chance to serve your community, for in those moments, you're not only making a difference in the lives of others but also honoring a divine calling to care for those around you.

Be Inspired: Make Bold Moves

DEVOTION 148

We See You, and More Importantly, God Sees You

IN OUR EFFORTS TO help our neighbors, it's crucial to recognize not only the visible needs but also the hearts and souls of those we serve. We might offer food, clothing, or shelter, but it's equally important to acknowledge the dignity and worth of every individual.

In 1 Samuel 16:7, God reminds us, "The LORD does not look at the things people look at. People look at the outward appearance, but the LORD looks at the heart." When we serve our neighbors, it's not just about the tangible support we provide. It's about seeing the person behind the need.

We often say, "We see you," to convey our acknowledgment of someone's presence. But beyond our gaze, there's a more profound truth: God sees them. He knows their struggles, their hopes, and their worth. When we engage in the work of helping our neighbors, we become instruments of God's love and compassion.

Through our actions, we demonstrate that God's love extends to every corner of our world. As you continue your efforts to help your neighbor, remember that your service is not just a physical act; it's a reflection of God's profound love and grace. You're showing that they matter, that they're seen, and that they're cherished, not just by you, but by the Creator of the universe. In this way, you're not only changing lives but also revealing the heart of God to those you serve.

Be Inspired: Make Bold Moves

DEVOTION 149

Victory: Claiming the Promised Land

IN DEUTERONOMY 20:16, WE find a verse that speaks of a profound concept: victory. It says, "But in the cities of these peoples that the LORD your God is giving you for an inheritance, you shall save alive nothing that breathes" (ESV). This verse is part of a larger context in the Bible, where the people of Israel were about to enter the Promised Land. It's a land promised to them, but it wasn't going to be a cakewalk. They would face battles and challenges.

This verse reminds us that victories often come after battles. It's a testament to the idea that we must sometimes overcome obstacles, fight our way through adversity, and persist through difficulties to claim the blessings and promises set before us.

In our own lives, we may encounter struggles and obstacles. There are times when the Promised Land, our goals, or our dreams seem just out of reach. But this verse encourages us not to give up. It's a reminder that victory comes to those who persevere, who continue to push forward even in the face of adversity.

Just as the people of Israel were given the Promised Land as their inheritance, we have promises, dreams, and goals set before us. The battles we face are part of the journey toward claiming those promises. When the journey gets tough, when obstacles seem insurmountable, remember this verse. Embrace the battles as opportunities to grow, to learn, and to draw closer to the victory that awaits.

Victory is often on the other side of challenges and struggles. Take heart, and with faith and determination, continue to move forward in your journey. Victory is not a question of "if" but "when" you persist and trust in the promises that are yours.

Be Inspired: Make Bold Moves

Full Armor: Equipped to Serve

Ephesians 6:13 reminds us of the importance of putting on the full armor of God:

"Therefore put on the full armor of God, so that when the day of evil comes, you may be able to stand your ground, and after you have done everything, to stand."

This verse is often associated with spiritual warfare, but its message extends to the work of a community servant and advocate as well. Just as a soldier equips themselves for battle, community servants equip themselves to stand up for what is right, just, and fair.

In community service and advocacy, you may face challenges, opposition, and difficult situations. It can sometimes feel like a battle. The full armor of God includes components like truth, righteousness, faith, salvation, and the Word of God. Let's apply these components to your role as a community servant:

1. **Truth.** Stand on the truth and transparency. Honesty and integrity are your allies. In a world filled with misinformation, being a source of truth is powerful.
2. **Righteousness.** Pursue justice and righteousness in all your actions. Advocate for what is fair and just, especially for those who are marginalized or oppressed.

3. **Faith.** Trust that your efforts can make a difference. Faith can move mountains, and it can also change communities for the better.
4. **Salvation.** Work to bring about change that leads to salvation, not just in a spiritual sense but also in a very practical sense. This might mean fighting for access to healthcare, education, or a fair justice system.
5. **Word of God.** Let your actions and words be guided by compassion, empathy, and love, much like the teachings in the Bible. Use them to inspire and motivate those around you.

Just as a soldier prepares for battle by putting on their armor, you prepare for your role as a community servant by equipping yourself with these virtues. When you face challenges, remember that you are not alone. The full armor of God surrounds you, and it empowers you to stand your ground, no matter the circumstances.

As you continue your work in the community, know that you are part of something greater. You are not just an individual; you are an embodiment of hope, change, and progress. With the full armor of God, you can stand strong, advocate for the vulnerable, and bring about a brighter future for all.

Be Inspired: Make Bold Moves

PART 2

Extra Content
from Gail's INSPIRE Series

1

Lucy Did It

DID YOU KNOW THAT on December 9, 1965, "A Charlie Brown Christmas" premiered, captivating half of the United States?

As I watched this classic on Apple TV, I noticed Lucy. Lucy, the ever-opinionated Peanuts character, ran a pop-up business—Psychiatric Help for just 5 cents. Charlie Brown was her client and learned the lesson of upfront payment.

Let's glean insights for our businesses from *INSPIRE: A Call to Action*, a Gail Dudley signature program.

1. BOLD BEGINNINGS

In 1965, Lucy showed us that boldness pays off. Embrace your uniqueness, and let your business stand out.

2. UPFRONT PAYMENT CONFIDENCE

Following Lucy's lead, ask for payment upfront. It sets the tone for the value you provide.

3. VISIBILITY MATTERS

Lucy had a sign; you should too. A clear company name and pricing help build trust and transparency.

4. ADAPTABILITY

Lucy adapted her business to the season as she cleared the snow from her booth. What needs clearing from your desk to work on and build your offerings, meeting the evolving needs of your clients?

5. THE ART OF BUSINESS RELATIONSHIPS

For Charlie Brown to sit at her table says something powerful. Remember, she would always remove the football when he was encouraged to run and kick it. However, there was a trust factor between him and Lucy. It's about building relationships. Build strong connections, prioritize your clients, and watch your business thrive.

Bottom line: If Lucy, a Peanuts character, did it, so can we!

Today's inspiration: Be bold. Shout about what you do. Get paid.[4]

---

[4] Gail Dudley, "Lucy Did It," https://gaildudley.medium.com/lucy-did-it-44db5e1a3daa.

2

Fund Raising 101

A CALL FOR COMMUNITY involvement and civic engagement. Whether you're a business owner, part of a nonprofit, building your personal brand, or engaged in ministry, the compass inevitably points back to the heartbeat of society—community engagement.

In the spirit of inspiration, consider the concept of building a social enterprise. Picture this: your business or personal brand intricately woven into the fabric of your local community. The possibilities are endless.

At READY Media, prior to the pandemic, our social enterprise focused on nurturing young minds through summer intensives for high school juniors and seniors passionate about writing and journalism. Students interacted with reporters, authors, journalists, and AP English teachers, crafting articles later published in *READY Publication*.

Similarly, with *News in Motion*, our social enterprise addresses food insecurity by partnering with organizations dedicated to this cause. Individually, advocacy extends from aiding authors and women's business owners to guiding seniors through Medicaid and Medicare, demystifying the voting process, and simplifying legislation understanding.

As year month or year unfolds, community, partnerships, social enterprises, and town halls emerges. The call for help is imminent, and our response lies in strategic fundraising.

Raise Funds for Communities: A Practical Guide

1. BUILD AN ADVISORY TEAM

Initiate by assembling a dedicated advisory team comprising 3–5 individuals. But, look beyond this core group for diverse perspectives.

2. GET TO KNOW THE COMMUNITY

Dive into the heart of your community. Understand its dynamics, challenges, and strengths.

3. ESTABLISH CONNECTION POINTS

Identify the center between you, your brand, business, or ministry and the community. What common ground can be cultivated?

4. DEVELOP A CASE STATEMENT (VISION FORWARD)

a. **Focus.** Clearly articulate the focal point of your initiative.
b. **Community Foundation.** Understand the essence of the community.
c. **History.** Explore the community's journey.
d. **Community Needs.** Identify the pressing needs.
e. **Entry Points and Connections.** Pinpoint areas for engagement.
f. **Training Needs.** Assess what skills or knowledge the community requires.

g. **Execution Plan.** Detail how your initiative will be implemented.

h. **Population Data.** Understand the demographic makeup.

i. **Volunteer Recruitment.** Develop strategies for garnering community support.

5. BUILD A DONORS LIST

Compile a comprehensive list of potential donors who resonate with your cause.

The call for community engagement awaits, and together, we can make a difference.

THE TITLE AND CHALLENGE

Let's talk about the title for a moment and dive into the realm of community care and social impact; let's add a touch of friendly challenge to the mix. You may be familiar with the phrase "I'll raise you..." commonly heard in card games. While we may not be avid bettors, let's leverage this concept in the spirit of giving back to our communities.

Picture this: a donor stepping up and saying, "I'll raise you..." pledging to match a certain amount of donations. It's a powerful commitment that magnifies the impact of every contribution. Now, imagine if we all embraced this challenge.

Are you ready? "I'll raise you..." becomes a call to action. Can we collectively rise to the occasion and magnify our efforts for the greater good? I believe we can. Let's kick off this challenge and watch as our collective contributions create a ripple effect of positive change.

Together, we can make a difference that transcends individual efforts. Let the spirit of community and generosity guide us on this impactful journey.

No fixed amount is required. Simply survey your community and match the generosity of a previous donor. Alternatively, rally three neighbors for a combined donation, or join forces with influencers or businesses for a friendly competition. By uniting our efforts, we can channel a substantial amount of funds into our communities.

3

Give the Gift of Voter Education

BIRTHDAY, ANNIVERSARY, GRADUATION, OR any holiday, consider giving a unique and invaluable gift—the gift of voter education. No monetary exchange is necessary; all that's required is a commitment to enlightening those who are not yet registered to vote on the significance of participating in the democratic process. Additionally, let's focus on educating registered voters about staying informed consistently, ensuring that every vote contributes to shaping our society.

Voting is not just a right; it is a powerful exercise of one's voice and civic duty. While protests remain a crucial aspect of our community fabric, imagine the impact if those who march for change first exercised their right to vote. In the United States, Pew Research found that around six-in-ten individuals (approximately 58%) express dissatisfaction with the direction of the country.[5] However, I wonder how many of these individuals are unregistered voters.

Similarly, Pew Research shows that Americans are not consistent voters based upon the chart found at this website.[6] Additionally, Census.gov records that among those who were registered, a common answer was "Too busy, conflicting work

---

[5] Andrew Daniller, "Americans take a dim view of the nation's future, look more positively at the past," Pew Research, last modified April 24, 2023, https://www.pewresearch.org/short-reads/2023/04/24/americans-take-a-dim-view-of-the-nations-future-look-more-positively-at-the-past/.

[6] "Voter Turnout, 2018-2022," Pew Research Center, last modified July 12, 2023, https://www.pewresearch.org/politics/2023/07/12/voter-turnout-2018-2022/.

or school schedule," leading them to abstain from voting. The bridge between not being registered and choosing not to vote lies in education.[7]

Understanding ballot measures, comprehending the legislative process, and recognizing the connection between bills and our daily lives are essential components of civic education. Perhaps there is a disconnect because we've lost touch with the stories of our great-grandparents and grandparents.

Growing up, I was surrounded by my grandparents, who shared tales of overcoming disparities and navigating the intricacies of making laws. My grandmother, for instance, insisted that the bank manager grant my grandfather a mortgage, armed with a cash-filled account. Her determination extended to becoming an election poll worker and casting an informed vote once granted the right.

Reflecting on the stories of my aunts and uncles, who gathered to teach people to read and write, I draw inspiration for my work today as a media advocate, publishing consultant, and policy architect. Much of my efforts, encapsulated in *News in Motion* from Monday to Thursday, aim to tell compelling stories that engage, educate, and empower individuals to cast informed ballots.

This holiday season, consider initiating loving conversations about voting while gathered around festive decorations, tables, or during family vacations. Steer clear of party affiliations and instead dive into topics such as economics, social justice, human rights, women's rights, children, education, and healthcare. Share personal stories from the past, connecting them to the reasons you vote and emphasizing the

---

[7] "2022 Voting and Registration Data Now Available," United States Census Bureau, last modified May 2, 2023, https://www.census.gov/newsroom/press-releases/2023/2022-voting-registration.html.

importance of voting. Encourage creativity and storytelling, making it a memorable and impactful experience.

This gift of voter education is one that will endure beyond the holiday season. As you gather, take the opportunity to discuss and understand the individual narratives that shape our perspectives on voting. Together, let's make a giving season a celebration of informed civic participation that resonates well into the future.

Conclusion

AS I CONCLUDE THIS devotional, it's vital to remember that making bold moves involves not only stepping out in faith but also discerning when to let go. There are moments when we must release control and place our trust in God's presence, purpose, and promises. It takes courage to walk this path, knowing that our God is unwaveringly faithful.

Embrace truth as your guiding light, for truth has the potential to set us free, even in these turbulent times. As the veils of falsehood are lifted and truth is unveiled, let us practice wisdom and discernment in our interactions. The power of truth, when paired with compassion and patience, holds the ability to heal wounds, dispel untruths, and illuminate hearts.

Recall the profound words from John 8:31-32: "If you stick with this, living out what I tell you, you are my disciples for sure. Then you will experience for yourselves the truth, and the truth will free you" (MSG). Therefore, let us move forward, sharing the truth in ways that mirror the love and compassion of Christ. Whether through bold stances or gentle conversations, may our actions align with God's timing and purpose.

Make room for what God has for you. This is your season to live life abundantly, embracing your journey of community service, advocacy, and the dissemination of truth. Your purpose is intricately woven into God's divine plan, and your influence has the potential to be transformative. Stay well, be resolute in making bold moves, and live life to its fullest potential.

The act of sharing truth is multifaceted, demanding various approaches. Sometimes it requires a steadfast and assertive stance, while at other times, it necessitates patience and a willingness to follow God's timetable. We are witnesses to a revelation, and it unfolds at precisely the right moment.

In our interactions, let's earnestly seek God's wisdom, exploring diverse methods to communicate with those who might be blinded or wounded by their circumstances. Our aim should never be to deceive but to spread truth and light.

As we navigate the vast sea of knowledge and consult different sources, may our circle of influence become a powerful catalyst for collective change, connecting God's eternal Word with the ever-evolving narratives of today. This is an exciting and potent undertaking.

I'm Gail Dudley, and this has been your *News in Motion*, conveyed through 150 Bold Moves devotionals, each designed to inspire. Be well, be bold, and live your life in abundance.

FOR THIS REASON

For this reason I kneel before the Father, from whom every family in heaven and on earth derives its name. I pray that out of his glorious riches he may strengthen you with power through his Spirit in your inner being, so that Christ may dwell in your hearts through faith. And I pray that you, being rooted and established in love, may have power, together with all the Lord's holy people, to grasp how wide and long and high and deep is the love of Christ, and to know this love that surpasses knowledge—that you may be filled to the measure of all the fullness of God (Ephesians 3:14-19).

Now to him who is able to do immeasurably more than all we ask or imagine, according to his power that is at work within us, to him be glory in the church and in Christ Jesus throughout all generations, for ever and ever! Amen (Ephesians 3:20-21).

Gail Dudley,
The Audacious Advocate

GAIL JOYFULLY INSPIRES AND connects with a diverse and dedicated community across various media platforms, where people, prayer, and politics intersect. For over two decades, she has been on a purposeful mission, inspiring and mobilizing individuals to reach their full potential.

As an expert in civic engagement, Gail has an awakening of the status quo and calls people to action. Gail boldly inspires and highlights entrepreneurs, nonprofits, causes, and political platforms through her media outlet as the influential host of *News in Motion*. With a loyal and engaged audience spanning multiple platforms, her mission is to uplift individuals and unlock their potential through inspiration and action.

Gail's unique intersection drives her to provoke, address controversial topics, dismantle complacency, and foster global dialogues, while leaving a positive impact on individuals, families, communities, and the world.

You can book her for an in-class session or interview her on your podcast or news segment today. Through her *News in Motion* show, Gail passionately champions entrepreneurs, nonprofits, causes, and political platforms.

News in Motion operates as an aggregated media platform, dedicated to fostering citizen engagement in civic life. By delivering headline news, voter education, and encouraging voter participation, it serves as a catalyst for action with an uplifting message. We aim to instill a sense of empowerment and motivation. This grassroots movement seeks to inspire individuals through informative and engaging content, encouraging them to take meaningful action in their communities and contribute to positive change.

www.ingramcontent.com/pod-product-compliance
Lightning Source LLC
Chambersburg PA
CBHW060322100426
42812CB00003B/858